This book is from

the kitchen library of

_____

_____

ALSO BY ART GINSBURG, MR. FOOD®

The **Mr. Food**® Cookbook, OOH IT'S SO GOOD!!™ (1990)

Mr. Food® Cooks Like Mama (1992)

Mr. Food® Cooks Chicken (1993)

Mr. Food® Cooks Pasta (1993)

Mr. Food® Makes Dessert (1993)

Mr. Food® Cooks Real American (1994)

Mr. Food®**'s** Favorite Cookies (1994)

Mr. Food®**'s** Quick and Easy Side Dishes (1995)

Mr. Food® Grills It All in a Snap (1995)

Mr. Food®**'s** Fun Kitchen Tips and Shortcuts (and Recipes, Too!) (1995)

Mr. Food®**'s** Old World Cooking Made Easy (1995)

"Help, **Mr. Food**®! Company's Coming!" (1995)

Mr. Food® Pizza 1-2-3 (1996)

Mr. Food® Meat Around the Table (1996)

Mr. Food® Simply Chocolate (1996)

Mr. Food® A Little Lighter (1996)

Mr. Food® From My Kitchen to Yours: Stories and Recipes from Home (1996)

Mr. Food® Easy Tex-Mex (1997)

Mr. Food® One Pot, One Meal (1997)

Mr. Food® Cool Cravings (1997)

Mr. Food®**'s** Italian Kitchen (1997)

Mr. Food®**'s** Simple Southern Favorites (1997)

Mr. Food®

A TASTE of QVC

Food & Fun Behind the Scenes

Art Ginsburg

Mr. Food®

WILLIAM MORROW AND COMPANY, INC.
NEW YORK

It is the policy of William Morrow and Company, Inc., and its imprints and affiliates, recog-
nizing the importance of preserving what has been written, to print the books we publish on
acid-free paper, and we exert our best efforts to that end.

Library of Congress Cataloging-in-Publication Data

Ginsburg, Art
    Mr. Food a taste of QVC : food & fun behind the scenes / Art Ginsburg, Mr. Food®.
        p.   cm.
    Includes index.
    ISBN 0-688-15897-8
    1. Cookery.   I. Title.
TX714.G572   1998   98-10169
641.5—dc21   CIP

Printed in the United States of America

First Edition

1   2   3   4   5   6   7   8   9   10

BOOK DESIGN BY MICHAEL MENDELSOHN OF MM DESIGN 2000, INC.

www.williammorrow.com
www.mrfood.com

Dedicated to
my loyal QVC viewers.
Cooking is much more fun when you
share the kitchen with me!
Thank you!

Foreword

They say the fastest way to a man's heart is through his stomach. I say the fastest way to my heart is through chocolate! So, when I met Mr. Food for the first time five years ago, and he fed me a heaping spoonful of Death by Chocolate, I lost my heart to him!

Mr. Food is exactly as he seems on television: warm, loving, and funny. You know how some people can light up a room? Mr. Food lights up the entire neighborhood! You know he is in the building because you can just feel his energy. I'll be on the air presenting silver jewelry or fashion, and Mr. Food will stop by behind the cameras to wave a cheery hello. This always puts a smile on my face, although the fact that a creamy cheesecake may not be far behind adds to my delight!

What sets Mr. Food apart from the crowd is that he truly cares about you, me, and everyone he meets. He has a big heart and lots of room in it for a huge extended family, especially where QVC is concerned. He proudly shows pictures of his grandkids and delights in the stories of your own precious little ones. That's what Mr. Food is all about: family. Sharing joys and laughter around a family table filled with delicious food is Mr. Food's idea of a five-star meal.

There have been many zany moments on the air with Mr. Food, and one of my favorites occurred during a huge snowstorm in January of 1996. It was freezing outside, snowing so fiercely that no one other than a polar bear would venture outside. Mr. Food thought it would be great fun to promote his upcoming show with a live shot from outside. So, out he ventured into the snow, waiting patiently for his turn to go on the air, then promoting his upcoming segment as his title on the screen read "Mr. FROZEN Food!" And I fondly recall the time he helped ease my hungry and pregnant tummy with a delicious chicken dish. Oh, then there was the time I confided I was entertaining in the afternoon, but was tired by my very early wake-up call. There appeared a chocolate chip Mr. Food cheesecake to delight me and my guests! And I think I have eaten more on the air with Mr. Food than with all the other cook shows I've hosted. His food is the best and "It's so good!!"

I not only have the honor of working with Mr. Food on QVC, I am one of his biggest fans! Many a Treacy family party has been capped off with Two-Minute Hawaiian Pie, a recipe I share every time I serve it. His books not only contain delicious recipes, they are fun to read! Plus, Mr. Food will never send you on a wild goose chase for exotic and expensive ingredients. His food is simple to prepare, but tastes like you've slaved over a hot stove all day! It's no surprise he is famous for the line *"OOH IT'S SO GOOD!!®"* because it always is!

Your meals can really be enhanced by recipes from the QVC family, represented in this wonderful cookbook. From Show Host favorites to Mr. Food classics, this is a book you will reach for time and time again. My wish is that this book is the start of many happy family meals for you.

As you must have realized by now, Mr. Food is one terrific guy in my eyes. That's due in part to the fact that I've worked with many people in my eleven years on QVC, and Mr. Food

shines as a genuine, talented, wonderful man. Whether he is on QVC, writing a new cookbook, or meeting some new fans at Studio Park, he never forgets the most important ingredient in food and in life: love.

We love you, Mr. Food!

—Jane Rudolph Treacy

Acknowledgments

Did you know that QVC is my "home away from home"? Why? Because of all the terrific people who make up the QVC family. And there were so many of them involved in making **Mr. Food**® *A Taste of QVC: Food & Fun Behind the Scenes* a reality . . . so many people who helped me compile my recipes and stories, along with photos, from my numerous exciting and enjoyable visits to QVC over the years. What better way to celebrate my fifth anniversary on the network?!

The enthusiastic QVC viewers are just the best, and I thank all those who shared their thoughts and recipes and encouraged me to create this book.

Doug Briggs, QVC President, inspires me with his ability to keep everything running smoothly in this enormous, successful organization; my thanks to Fred Siegel, Senior Vice President—Marketing; Jack Comstock, Vice President—Television Sales; Karen Fonner, Paula Piercy, and Larry Chilnick for continually challenging me to create more quick-and-easy cookbooks.

My appreciation extends to every department of QVC, from Ginger March, Stephanie Fallon, and Tammy Kriebel in Marketing and Promotion to Neal Grabell in Legal, QVC photographer Will Rutledge, and, of course, all the QVC hosts, from the veterans to the "new kids on the block." Thanks, also, to Sue Schick and Jo Ann Kurz for helping me pull everything together, and to the behind-the-scenes crew, from the planners, directors, and producers to the camera and telephone operators. What a team!

I owe a big thank-you to the QVC celebrity guests, who add real spark to the QVC programs and were most gracious in sharing their favorite family recipes and stories with me.

That's only the beginning! There are so many people to thank at William Morrow, my publisher. There's Bill Wright, President and CEO of the Hearst Book Group; Paul Fedorko, Publisher and Senior Vice President; Senior Editor Zachary Schisgal; and Assistant Editor Anne Cole. Richard Aquan, Nikki Basilone, Michael Murphy, and Jackie Deval play important roles in making our books come together, too, as do Designer Michael Mendelsohn and Illustrator Philip Scheuer.

I'd like to express special thanks to my agent, Bill Adler, for making this and all my books more than just a vision.

And speaking of visions, I bet you noticed the color pictures of a number of the dishes in this book. I want to thank Dave Tinsch of Fashion Plates for making everything look just right for these photos, skillfully done at The Hal Silverman Studio. What a great bunch of professionals they are! A hearty thank-you to Hal, Rick Needle, Frank Schram, and Nancy Nosiglia.

Then there's the fabulous Mr. Food team. That's where it all starts, you know—with my test kitchen crew. Once again I tip my chef's hat to Patty Rosenthal, the good-humored veteran of my kitchen; Janice Bruce, who's always full of fresh and novel ideas; Cheryl Gerber, who spreads sunshine on every recipe as well as on all of us; Cela Goodhue, who's as committed and dependable as can be; Ava Ray Bernardi, whose sense of style guarantees that everything looks fantastic; and Joan Wolff, who strives to find ways to keep my recipes light and tasty.

Joe Peppi heads up my test kitchen and documents every step

of each recipe. Skillfully assisting him is Charlie Tallant. And with her never-ending enthusiasm and determination, Larissa Lalka helped tweak my thoughts about each recipe.

I also want to thank my ever-supportive wife, Ethel; my lively administrative assistant, Marilyn Ruderman; my two sons—Steve, who manages the company along with me, and Chuck, who, with his assistant, Alice Palombo, keeps us on track with our 150-plus TV stations; my creative script assistant, Helayne Rosenblum; my exacting editorial assistant, Carol Ginsburg; and my customer service supervisor, Beth Ives.

When it comes to numbers, Chet Rosenbaum keeps us all in line. Tom Palombo heads the Mr. Food Sales and Licensing division, while his assistant, Heidi Triveri, watches over every detail. And if you've ever called our offices, you've been greeted by our cheerful receptionist, Robin Steiner.

I'll wrap up my thank-yous by saying that I truly appreciate the fine job done by Howard Rosenthal and my daughter, Caryl Ginsburg Fantel. With their boundless energy, these two handle each book project for me, overseeing the recipes from their inception to their final stage and coordinating the book design, photography, production, and on and on!

I thank each of you, and the following wonderful companies and individuals, and wish you all health, happiness, and strength as we journey on toward more books and, of course, more "OOH IT'S SO GOOD!!®"

Dairy Management Inc.
MIRRO/WEAREVER
David E. Muñoz, D.V.M., Cypress Wood Animal Hospital
National Cattlemen's Beef Association

Contents

A Moderate Approach

Cooking lighter doesn't mean changing your whole lifestyle. All you have to do is follow a few basic steps and you'll be ready to enjoy healthier eating. Here are a few ideas to help you substitute lighter ingredients in your everyday cooking. With a little moderation, together we'll enjoy many more years together of "OOH IT'S SO GOOD!!®"

Chicken	In most recipes, you can substitute boneless, skinless chicken breasts for whole chicken or parts. Remember that boneless breasts are generally thinner, so they'll cook more quickly than bone-in parts; adjust your cooking times accordingly.
Dairy	Let's look to our supermarket dairy case for some reduced-fat, low-fat, or fat-free alternatives. For instance, there's low-fat milk for our soups and sauces, instead of heavy cream. (Evaporated skim milk will work, too.)
Cream Cheese	Easy—use light or fat-free cream cheese!
Mozzarella Cheese	Many of the low-fat and part-skim mozzarella cheeses taste just as good as the traditional types. They're perfect alternatives, plus you can usually cut down on the amount you use. (We can often reduce the amount of cheese we sprinkle on the tops of casseroles without anybody even noticing!)
Parmesan Cheese	Parmesan is an excellent choice when watch-

ing fat and calories, since its strong flavor means that a little goes a long way! (It's the same with Romano cheese.)

Ricotta Cheese	For rich taste while still watching fat, in most ricotta recipes you can use half regular ricotta and half light or fat-free ricotta. Or, don't hesitate to use all light or fat-free. The choice is yours.
Sour Cream	I often use light versions without missing any flavor, but because sour cream varies widely by brand, I recommend trying several brands until you find the one with the taste and consistency you like best.
Whipped Cream	Many desserts call for whipped cream or whipped topping. To watch calories and fat with those, we've got great choices available with reduced-fat and nonfat whipped toppings. You may need to increase the flavoring or sugar a bit, though, depending on the recipe.
Dressings	Add a splash of vinegar or citrus juice— lemon, lime, or orange—to dressings, marinades, vegetables, poultry, almost anything —to wake up your taste buds.
Eggs	In many cases, we can replace whole eggs with egg whites. (Two egg whites equal one whole egg.) And, yes, in most recipes, you can go ahead and replace eggs altogether with egg substitute. (It's usually available near the eggs in the refrigerated section of the supermarket.) However, I don't recommend using egg substitute when coating

foods for breading. Breading doesn't stick to it very well.

Mayonnaise

When it comes to mayonnaise, there are lighter varieties available, too. And when using it in a salad, mix it in just before serving . . . you can usually get by with using less that way. Or sometimes I use a combination of half mayonnaise and half low-fat yogurt. It does the trick, too!

Meats

- Choose lean cuts of meat and trim away any visible fat before preparing.
- Serve moderate-sized portions, such as 3 to 4 ounces of cooked meat (4 to 6 ounces raw) per adult. (That's about the size of a deck of playing cards.)
- Choose cooking methods (like roasting, broiling, grilling, and baking on a rack) that allow fat to drip away during cooking.
- Remove the layer of fat that rises to the top of soups, stews, and the pan juices of roasts. Chilling makes this a breeze, so it's even easier to do with dishes that are made ahead and chilled before being reheated. Or, a timesaving tip for removing fat from soups and stews is to simply add a few ice cubes to the warm cooked dish. As soon as the fat sticks to the cubes, remove them, and the fat will come out right along with them!

Ground Beef and Pork

- Select a very lean blend, preferably with a 90 to 10 ratio of lean meat to fat. (Regular ground beef and pork usually have a 70 to 30 ratio.)

- If browning ground beef or pork before adding it to a recipe, after browning, place it in a strainer and rinse it with warm water, then drain and continue as directed. This should remove most of the excess fat.
- In most recipes, you can replace ground beef or pork with turkey. Keep in mind, though, that ground turkey needs more seasoning than beef or pork.

Sausage   Many markets now offer a variety of lean sausages. This means that there's less fat mixed in with the meat when the sausage is made. Other alternatives to traditional pork or beef sausage are turkey and chicken sausages. Whichever way you go, be sure to read the nutrition label so you know your fat and calorie savings.

Nuts   When a recipe calls for nuts, don't be afraid to cut down the amount. Usually we can cut the amount in half and still get great flavor and texture.

Oils   Select oils such as canola or safflower for frying; they're lower in saturated fat than other types.

Sauces   Have you seen all the tomato sauces and other tomato products available in the supermarket lately? Not only are there lots of flavors available, but most manufacturers are offering sauces that have less fat and calories, and even ones with less sodium, too. Some of these may be thinner than our "regular" sauces, so you may want to use a bit less of them in casseroles.

Soups Canned soups are a great beginning for sauces and casseroles. If we choose lighter or reduced-fat or reduced-sodium versions, we can sure save calories and cut down on fat and sodium.

How you eat is almost as important as *what* you eat. So follow these basic common-sense eating habits:

- Eat regularly scheduled meals and limit eating between meals. There are two rules of thumb on this: Eat three scheduled meals a day and limit eating between meals *OR* eat five to six light meals throughout the day. But don't do both, and *never* stuff yourself!
- Try not to eat within two hours of bedtime.
- Watch portion sizes! Smaller portions mean fewer calories, so serve yourself only as much food as you think you'll eat. It's okay to leave some on your plate, too.

A Note About Packaged Foods

Packaged food sizes may vary by brand. Generally, the sizes indicated in these recipes are average sizes. If you can't find the exact package size listed in the ingredients, whatever package is closest in size will usually do the trick.

Recipe Contents

BREADS

BRUNCH

SANDWICHES AND PIZZAS

PASTA

DRINKS

DESSERTS

HODGEPODGE

Preface

It all started a few years ago on a partly cloudy spring day—May 28, 1993, to be exact. I appeared on QVC for the first time. You see, my first two cookbooks, *The Mr. Food® Cookbook, OOH IT'S SO GOOD!!™* and *Mr. Food® Cooks Like Mama*, were some of the first books ever sold on QVC.

What an honor that was! I remember it so clearly. The show was called *Now You're Cooking*, and I appeared with my now–old friend Jane Rudolph Treacy. At the time, I was more than a little nervous. What if none of my books sold?!

My segment was scheduled to be twelve minutes long, but after just a few whirlwind minutes we went to a break. I thought I must have really bombed! Imagine my surprise when they told me we had to cut the segment short because my books had sold out!

Fortunately, that first QVC experience was a good one . . . so good that I've returned many times since then, offering my first two books as well as twenty new cookbook titles! Yup, that day in May was a turning point for me. It showed me that there are lots of great people out there who really want quick and easy no-nonsense recipes and tips.

And even though I'm a regular on QVC, I still get a little bit of that nervous feeling in my stomach before I go on the air. But it doesn't last long, 'cause the hosts and all my other QVC friends sure do help me feel at home.

During these past years I've worked with just about every

QVC host, made many new behind-the-scenes friends, and prepared many tasty recipes to share. I'm happy to say that we've become like family. So in case you missed my debut, I decided to take everybody back to sample my very first QVC recipes. It's sort of my own version of "Mr. Food, the Early Years." Enjoy!

Preface

Grilled Honey-Garlic Pork Chops

6 servings

On my first visit to QVC, I couldn't believe how enthusiastic the viewers were. I mean, with all the cookbooks in the world, they were anxious to get mine. I later realized why—because all the ingredients I use are easily available, the recipes are tasty, and we can throw them together in a snap. I think these pork chops demonstrate all this pretty well, don't you?

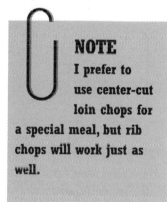

NOTE
I prefer to use center-cut loin chops for a special meal, but rib chops will work just as well.

¾ cup lemon juice

¾ cup honey

⅓ cup soy sauce

3 tablespoons dry sherry or dry white wine

6 garlic cloves, minced

6 pork loin chops (2 to 2½ pounds total), about ¾ inch thick (see Note)

In a 9" × 13" baking dish, combine all the ingredients except the pork chops; mix well. Add the pork chops. Cover and marinate for at least 8 hours, or overnight, in the refrigerator, turning occasionally. Preheat the grill to medium heat. Discard the marinade and grill the chops for about 10 minutes per side, or until cooked through.

Better Baked Ziti

6 to 8 servings

Who doesn't love a big steaming dish of pasta, loaded with sauce and smothered in oodles of cheese? I know it was a favorite of Jane Rudolph Treacy's during my first QVC appearance. Why, it's become a favorite of my family's, too, and I serve it pretty often at our get-togethers. It's a special dish 'cause it can be made ahead and reheated. And it always tastes great, no matter when we make it!

½ pound ziti
1 container (15 ounces) ricotta cheese
3 cups (12 ounces) shredded mozzarella cheese, divided
1 jar (28 ounces) spaghetti sauce
½ cup grated Parmesan cheese

NOTE
Use your favorite type of flavored spaghetti sauce to add additional flavor to this ziti. And don't worry if you don't have ziti on hand—just substitute any other equal-sized shape.

Preheat the oven to 350°F. Coat a 9" × 13" baking dish with nonstick cooking spray. Cook the ziti according to the package directions; drain and place in a large bowl. Add the ricotta cheese and 1½ cups mozzarella cheese; mix well. Spread half of the spaghetti sauce over the bottom of the baking dish. Spoon the ziti mixture into the dish; cover with the remaining spaghetti sauce. Sprinkle with the Parmesan cheese and top with the remaining 1½ cups mozzarella cheese. Bake for 25 to 30 minutes, or until heated through and the cheese is golden.

Oriental Steak

4 to 6 servings

Since the debut of my first set of books, I've gotten requests for recipes that follow this fad or that one. But one request that's been constant over the years is the one for "big bold flavors," so it's easy to see why this recipe's an old favorite that still tops my request list.

½ cup soy sauce
2 tablespoons honey
2 tablespoons cider vinegar
2 tablespoons sesame oil
¼ teaspoon ground ginger
2 garlic cloves, minced
One 2½- to 3-pound boneless beef steak (flank, chuck, sirloin, or round)
2 tablespoons browning and seasoning sauce

In a small bowl, combine all the ingredients except the steak and browning and seasoning sauce; mix well. Place the steak in a large resealable plastic storage bag. Add the marinade and seal the bag. Marinate in the refrigerator for 3 to 4 hours, or overnight, turning occasionally. Preheat the broiler. Place the steak on a broiling pan; discard the marinade. Brush with the browning and seasoning sauce and broil for 7 to 9 minutes per side for medium, or until desired doneness beyond that. Cut across the grain into thin slices and serve.

NOTE
For an easy change of pace, sometimes I use vegetable oil instead of sesame oil and bottled garlic instead of fresh, add a few shakes of hot pepper sauce, and use bottled sweet-and-sour sauce instead of honey.

Two-Minute Hawaiian Pie

6 to 8 servings

We all know what it's like to have guests drop in unexpectedly or to be invited to a last-minute potluck meal. Well, here's a simple solution to the last-minute dessert dilemma—a two-minute pie with just four ingredients, plus easy garnishes. This tropical treat looks so good that nobody will believe you made it in just two minutes! (Yup, it's that easy . . . that's why it went over so well as the first recipe I demonstrated on QVC!)

1 can (20 ounces) crushed pineapple in syrup, undrained
1 package (6-serving size) instant vanilla pudding and pie filling (see Note)
1 container (8 ounces) sour cream
One 9-inch prepared shortbread pie crust
1 can (8 ounces) sliced pineapple, drained and halved
8 maraschino cherries, drained
2 tablespoons sweetened flaked coconut

NOTE
Don't make the vanilla pudding according to the package directions; just add the dry instant pudding mix right to the other ingredients.

In a large bowl, combine the crushed pineapple with its syrup, the pudding mix, and sour cream; mix until well blended. Spoon into the pie crust and decorate the top with the sliced pineapple and cherries; sprinkle with the coconut. Cover and chill for at least 2 hours before serving.

Death by Chocolate

serves up to 24 (or 1 serious chocoholic!)

This is by far the most requested Mr. Food recipe of all time. Chocoholics around the country swear by it. I remember watching the producers holding back the crowd that had gathered in the studio the day this recipe debuted. I thought they were trying to keep everybody quiet, but they were actually trying to get first dibs. In fact, I think this recipe might just be the reason my first books sold out so quickly. The best part? Death by Chocolate tastes just as good as it looks—and it's so easy to prepare.

1 package (21 ounces) brownie mix, batter prepared according to the package directions

¼ cup coffee-flavored liqueur (see Note)

2 packages (2.8 ounces each) instant chocolate mousse, prepared according to the package directions (see Note)

8 (1.4-ounce) chocolate-covered toffee candy bars (like Skor® or Heath®), coarsely crushed

1 container (12 ounces) frozen whipped topping, thawed

NOTE
Break the candy bars into small pieces in a food processor or by gently tapping the wrapped bars with a hammer. Instead of the coffee liqueur, you can use a mixture of 1 teaspoon sugar and ¼ cup leftover black coffee, or leave out the coffee flavoring entirely. And instead of instant chocolate mousse, you can prepare two 4-serving packages of instant chocolate pudding.

Preheat the oven and bake the brownie batter in a 9" × 13" baking pan according to the package directions; allow to cool completely. Use a fork to prick holes in the top of the cooled brownies; drizzle with the coffee liqueur. Break up the brownies into small pieces and place half in the bottom of a trifle dish or large glass serving bowl. Cover with half of the mousse, then one third of the crushed candy and half of the whipped topping. Repeat the layers and top with the remaining crushed candy. Cover and chill for at least 2 hours before serving.

A Host of Recipes

One of the things I like best about visiting QVC is the people. And let me tell you, the program hosts are truly as nice off the air as they appear on camera. Over the years, we've all grown together and shared many a good time.

When I started putting together my ideas for this book, there was no question that I had to include recipes from all my QVC host friends. Due to our busy schedules, the time we spend together is often brief—and most of it is spent discussing food! So I've heard about many of their family recipes and all-

Checking in with QVC buddy Sue Schick

time favorite meals and desserts. And boy, were they ever excited about sharing them with me—and you! Now it's your turn to enjoy these stories, pictures, and, most of all, recipes from your friends and mine at QVC.

A Host of Recipes

A Host of Recipes

Patricia Bastia

4 to 6 servings

Southern Chicken and Biscuits

Patricia grew up watching the Mr. Food show on the local news in Providence, Rhode Island. She sure learned how to prepare some quick throw-together meals—and this chicken and biscuits dish is the successful result of her own experimenting with her family! You know, she's even prepared it loads of times during her cooking segments on QVC.

1 can (14½ ounces) ready-to-use chicken broth
¼ cup (½ stick) butter
½ teaspoon black pepper
1½ pounds boneless, skinless chicken breasts,
    cut into 1-inch chunks
2 packages (10.8 ounces each) refrigerated biscuits
    (5 biscuits each)
½ teaspoon paprika
½ cup chopped fresh parsley

In a large skillet, combine the broth, butter, and pepper; add the chicken chunks and cook over medium-high heat for 5 minutes, or until bubbly. Place the biscuits evenly over the top. Reduce the heat to low, cover, and cook for 10 minutes. Sprinkle with the paprika and simmer, uncovered, for 10 to 12 minutes, or until the broth is slightly thickened. Sprinkle with the parsley and serve.

DID YOU KNOW . . .

Patricia's acting credits include appearances in *L.A. Law, Picket Fences, Our Town,* and *West Side Story?* In her spare time, she enjoys cooking (hooray!), gardening, and playing the piano.

12

Jill Bauer

12 to 15 squares

Lemon Squares

Jill tells me she has a big sweet tooth and one of her favorite treats is lemon squares. She said, "These are the best I've ever tried and I hope you enjoy them!" Thanks, Jill, I'm sure we *all* will!

2½ cups all-purpose flour, divided
1 cup (2 sticks) butter or margarine, softened
1 cup confectioners' sugar, plus extra for topping
2 cups granulated sugar
4 eggs
½ cup lemon juice
1 teaspoon lemon extract

Preheat the oven to 350°F. In a medium bowl, combine 2 cups flour, the butter, and confectioners' sugar; mix until crumbly. Press into the bottom of a 9" × 13" baking dish to form a crust. Bake for 15 minutes. Meanwhile, in a large bowl, with an electric beater on medium speed, beat the remaining ½ cup flour, the granulated sugar, eggs, lemon juice, and lemon extract until well blended. Pour over the hot crust. Bake for 25 to 30 minutes, or until set. Allow to cool, then cut into squares. Dust with extra confectioners' sugar and serve.

DID YOU KNOW . . .

Jill is a former Irvine, California, Junior Miss? Here's what she has to say about being a show host: "After doing all the research, attending all the meetings, and doing all the studying that goes into hosting just those three hours on air, you tie it all together by simply being yourself."

Bob Bowersox

6 to 8 servings

Sweet-and-Sour Chicken

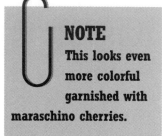

NOTE
This looks even more colorful garnished with maraschino cherries.

You've probably seen Bob and me sharing the QVC kitchen set many times. Yup, we go way back. What you *don't* see is the two of us backstage trading recipes, hints, and ideas when we're off camera. So, of course, Bob was happy to provide me with his yummy sweet-and-sour chicken recipe for this chapter. (Check out how colorful it is on color page K.)

2 tablespoons vegetable oil

2½ pounds boneless, skinless chicken breasts, cut into thin strips

1 can (20 ounces) pineapple chunks in syrup, drained and liquid reserved

1 can (8 ounces) sliced water chestnuts, drained

1 cup fresh broccoli florets

1 medium red bell pepper, cut into ¾-inch chunks

2 tablespoons soy sauce

1 tablespoon white vinegar

1 tablespoon ketchup

2 tablespoons cornstarch

2 tablespoons sugar

1 cup fresh snow peas, trimmed

14

Heat the oil in a large skillet or wok over high heat. Add the chicken and stir-fry for 4 to 5 minutes, or until no pink remains. Add the pineapple chunks, water chestnuts, broccoli, and red pepper. Stir-fry for 3 to 4 minutes, or until the vegetables are crisp-tender. In a small bowl, combine the reserved pineapple liquid, the soy sauce, vinegar, ketchup, cornstarch, and sugar; mix well. Stir into the skillet or wok and cook for 3 minutes. Add the snow peas and cook for 1 minute, or until the sauce has thickened. Serve immediately.

DID YOU KNOW . . .

Bob appeared on QVC's first broadcast? His knowledge of electronics, entertainment, and journalism and his love of cooking are what make Bob such a well-rounded show host.

Bob shares his love of food with wife Toni.

Steve Bryant

6 to 8 servings

Snickers® Cheesecake

Leave it to Steve! While getting ready for one of his shows, he was trying out a new heavy-duty mixer and he came up with this cheesecake that works like a charm every time. And the best part is that we don't even need the oven. By the way, the mixer was a sellout . . . and this cake will be, too!

2 packages (8 ounces each) cream cheese, softened
½ cup sugar
1 teaspoon vanilla extract
1 cup (½ pint) heavy cream
5 Snickers® candy bars (2.07 ounces each), coarsely
    chopped, divided
One 9-inch prepared graham cracker pie crust

In a large bowl, with an electric beater on medium speed, beat the cream cheese, sugar, and vanilla until smooth. In a medium bowl, with an electric beater on high speed, beat the heavy cream until stiff peaks form. Fold the whipped cream into the cream cheese mixture until well combined. Mix in 4 chopped candy bars. Spoon into the pie crust and top with the remaining chopped candy bar. Cover and chill overnight.

DID YOU KNOW . . .

Steve is an accomplished musician? He plans to release a CD featuring his original acoustic rock and is also the author of a number of books. What a creative guy!

Judy Crowell

about 2¼ cups

Artichoke Dip

Judy claims to be "not much of a cook," but once I tasted this dip I had to disagree. It's an appetizer that she likes to bring to parties, and Judy says she always comes home with an empty dish, practically licked clean. According to Judy, "It's down, dirty, quick, easy, and enjoyed by all."

1 can (14 ounces) artichoke hearts, drained and chopped
1 cup mayonnaise
1 cup grated Parmesan cheese
1 garlic clove, minced

NOTE
Judy suggests that we serve this with chips, crackers, or even cut-up fresh veggies.

Preheat the oven to 350°F. In a large bowl, combine all the ingredients; mix well. Pour into a small casserole dish and bake for 30 to 35 minutes, or until heated through and golden on top.

DID YOU KNOW . . .

Judy considers her hometown "Everywhere, USA"? She was born in Camp Zama, Japan, but since her father was in the army she's called four countries and twelve states home!

Paul Deasy

1 dozen fajitas

Chicken Fajitas

Paul is kind of "the new kid on the block." He says that since he's so busy, he rarely has time to cook—so when he *does* cook, it better be quick and easy. And nothing is quicker than his fajita recipe. It's a whole tasty meal wrapped in a tortilla. Now *that's* fast!

½ cup fresh lime juice

3 tablespoons vegetable oil, divided

4 teaspoons soy sauce

4 garlic cloves, minced

1 teaspoon chili powder

1 teaspoon ground red pepper

2 teaspoons salt

6 boneless, skinless chicken breast halves
   (1½ to 2 pounds total)

2 medium onions, thinly sliced

Twelve 8-inch flour tortillas, warmed

In a large glass bowl, combine the lime juice, 2 tablespoons oil, the soy sauce, garlic, chili powder, red pepper, and salt; mix well. Set aside ¼ cup of the marinade, then add the chicken to the remaining marinade. Cover and allow to marinate in the refrigerator for 2 hours. Heat the remaining

1 tablespoon oil in a large skillet over medium-high heat. Add the onions and sauté for 4 to 5 minutes, or until tender. Add the reserved marinade and cook for 3 to 4 minutes, or until the onions are browned. Transfer to a serving plate and cover with aluminum foil to keep warm. Add the chicken to the skillet, discarding the marinade, and cook the chicken for 7 to 8 minutes per side, or until no pink remains. Transfer to a cutting board and thinly slice, then place over the onions. Make fajitas by placing some of the chicken and onion mixture on each tortilla and rolling them.

NOTE
Before rolling the tortillas, you might want to add some shredded cheese, sour cream, diced red bell peppers, and/or salsa.

DID YOU KNOW . . .
Paul was the captain of the Cheerleading Squad at his alma mater, Penn State?

Rick Domeier

6 to 8 servings

Lasagna for Lovers

A newlywed, Rick says he's an expert on romance—and he promises that serving this lasagna is a guarantee of romance. He insists that it's best served with homemade bread, the red wine of your choice, candlelight, and soft music. It sounds like a perfect evening to me . . .

1 pound extra-lean ground turkey breast

2 medium onions, diced

2 tablespoons minced garlic

1 medium zucchini, cut into ½-inch chunks

¾ pound fresh mushrooms, sliced

1¼ cups tomato sauce

¾ cup crushed tomatoes

2 tablespoons tomato paste

¼ cup chopped fresh Italian parsley

15 fresh basil leaves and 6 chopped fresh basil leaves

1 teaspoon dried oregano

1 teaspoon salt

½ teaspoon black pepper

1 container (15 ounces) nonfat ricotta cheese

2 cups (8 ounces) shredded nonfat mozzarella cheese, divided

9 oven-ready no-boil lasagna noodles

Preheat the oven to 350°F. Coat a 9" × 13" baking dish with nonstick cooking spray. In a large nonstick skillet, cook the turkey, onions, and garlic over medium heat for 5 to 7 minutes, or until the turkey is no longer pink and the onions are tender, stirring to break up the turkey as it cooks; remove from the skillet and set aside. Coat the skillet with nonstick cooking spray; add the zucchini and mushrooms and sauté over medium heat for 5 to 7 minutes, or until tender. Add the tomato sauce, crushed tomatoes, tomato paste, parsley, the chopped basil, the oregano, salt, and pepper and simmer for 2 minutes, stirring constantly. Return the turkey mixture to the skillet; mix well and remove from the heat. In a small bowl, combine the ricotta cheese and 1½ cups mozzarella cheese; mix well. Spread 1 cup of the turkey mixture evenly over the bottom of the baking dish. Place 3 noodles evenly over it, then top with one third of the cheese mixture, 5 basil leaves, and 1 cup of the turkey mixture. Repeat the layers two more times, ending with the turkey mixture. Sprinkle the remaining ½ cup mozzarella cheese evenly over the top and cover with aluminum foil. Bake for 35 minutes; uncover and bake for 5 to 10 more minutes, or until bubbly and the top is golden.

NOTE
To keep the cheese from sticking to the aluminum foil during baking, spray some nonstick cooking spray on the side of the foil that will come in contact with the cheese.

DID YOU KNOW . . .

Rick has appeared on various TV shows, including *St. Elsewhere*, *Likely Suspects*, and *The Young and the Restless?* Maybe that's where he learned to be so romantic! I guess we should ask his bride, Amy.

Dan Hughes

4 to 6 servings

Stuffed Meat Loaf

On the many mornings spent with Dan on *The QVC Morning Show*, we've had lots of time to talk about food—both his favorite recipes and mine! He told me that one of his favorite meals was meat loaf and mashed potatoes, and he wished he could combine the two. Well, I gave Dan some pointers and look what he came up with!

> ¾ cup instant mashed potato flakes
>
> ½ cup warm water
>
> ¼ cup sour cream
>
> ¼ teaspoon salt
>
> 1½ pounds ground beef
>
> 4 scallions, finely chopped
>
> ½ cup seasoned bread crumbs
>
> ½ cup milk
>
> ½ cup ketchup, divided
>
> 2 garlic cloves, minced
>
> 1 egg
>
> 1 teaspoon black pepper

Preheat the oven to 350°F. In a medium bowl, combine the potato flakes, water, sour cream, and salt; mix well and set aside. In another medium bowl, combine the ground beef, scallions, bread crumbs, milk, ¼ cup ketchup, the garlic, egg, and pepper; mix well. Press half of the beef mixture into the bottom of a 5" × 9" loaf pan; using a spoon, press a ½-inch-deep indentation into the center, leaving a ½-inch border around the edges. Place the potato mixture in the indentation. Carefully place the remaining meat mixture over the potato mixture, sealing the edges. Brush the remaining ¼ cup ketchup evenly over the top. Bake for 55 to 60 minutes, or until the juices run clear; drain. Allow to sit for 5 minutes, then slice and serve.

DID YOU KNOW . . .

Dan loves a challenge? A real race fan, he enjoys hosting QVC's *For Race Fans Only*, where he even got to drive the Winston Cup Race Car! He must be pretty brave, since he's also toured the comedy club circuit from Indianapolis to San Francisco as a stand-up comic.

Pat James-DeMentri

12 to 15 servings

Mom's Apple Cake

As a former model and actress, Pat has many memories of unusual assignments—like the time she roller skated through New York City's Lincoln Tunnel for a jeans commercial. Even though that sounds like an exciting time, Pat says her favorite memories are of the times when her mom made her homemade apple cake; she especially loved the aroma that filled the house when it was baking. Pat was glad to share the recipe so that we can all create our own happy memories.

> 2 cups sliced McIntosh apples
> 1 cup granulated sugar
> ½ cup vegetable oil
> 2 eggs, beaten
> 1½ cups all-purpose flour
> 1 teaspoon baking soda
> ½ teaspoon ground cinnamon
> ½ teaspoon salt
> 2 tablespoons confectioners' sugar

Preheat the oven to 350°F. Coat a 9" × 13" baking dish with nonstick cooking spray. In a medium bowl, combine the apples and granulated sugar; mix well. Cover and allow to sit for 10 minutes. In a small bowl, combine the oil and eggs; mix well, then add to the apple mixture and stir until well combined. In another medium bowl, combine the flour, baking soda, cinnamon, and salt; mix well. Add to the apple mixture; mix well and pour into the baking dish. Bake for 30 to 35 minutes, or until a wooden toothpick inserted in the center comes out clean. Allow to cool, then sprinkle with the confectioners' sugar. Cut into squares and serve.

DID YOU KNOW . . .

Pat has a green thumb? She enjoys planting flowers and reading, but, more than anything, she loves curling up with her husband, her cat, and the "apple of her eye," daughter Nicole Anna.

Bonnie Johnson

4 to 6 servings

Turkey Chili

Bonnie tells me she loves to travel, read, and cook healthy. And because this recipe uses lean ground turkey breast, it fits the bill for healthy eating. You know, Bonnie likes her chili extra spicy, so this is guaranteed to knock your socks off. Of course, you can add or subtract chili powder and crushed red pepper to make it to your own taste. Remember—there are no rules.

1 tablespoon olive oil
1 pound lean ground turkey breast
1 large onion, coarsely chopped
1 can (15 ounces) tomato sauce
1 can (15 ounces) chili beans, undrained
½ cup water
¼ cup ketchup
2 tablespoons chili powder
2 tablespoons all-purpose flour
1 tablespoon sugar
½ teaspoon onion powder
½ teaspoon crushed red pepper
½ teaspoon salt

NOTE
This looks nice sprinkled with thinly sliced scallions just before serving. And go ahead and use any of your other favorite chili toppers, too.

Heat the oil in a soup pot over medium heat. Add the ground turkey and onion and sauté for 4 to 5 minutes, or until the turkey is browned and the onion is tender, stirring constantly. Add the remaining ingredients; mix well and bring to a boil. Reduce the heat to low, cover, and simmer for 50 to 60 minutes, or until thickened, stirring occasionally.

DID YOU KNOW . . .

one of the places Bonnie loves to travel to is North Carolina? She happily reports that her parents still live in the house she grew up in. What great memories . . .

Paul Kelley

6 to 8 servings

Kelley's French Onion–Mustard Pie

Since Paul's in charge of QVC's 50 in 50 Tour, you can bet he spends most of his time on the road. He wears many hats, one of them a chef's hat, which he happily dons to make his French Onion–Mustard Pie. Hopefully, someday he'll stop by the Mr. Food studio and make his specialty for me.

2 tablespoons butter
6 medium onions, thinly sliced
1 package (4.4 ounces) Boursin® herb cheese spread
1 cup sour cream
2 eggs
2 tablespoons Dijon-style mustard
2 tablespoons minced garlic
1 folded refrigerated pie crust (from a 15-ounce package)
½ pound Gruyère cheese, shredded

Preheat the oven to 350°F. In a soup pot, melt the butter over medium heat. Add the onions and sauté for 8 to 10 minutes, or until tender. In a medium bowl, with an electric beater on medium speed, beat the cheese spread, sour cream, eggs, mustard, and garlic until smooth. Unfold the pie crust and place in a 9-inch deep-dish pie plate, pressing the crust firmly into the plate. Place the onions in the pie crust and pour the cheese mixture over them. Sprinkle with the Gruyère cheese and bake for 45 to 50 minutes, or until golden and set. Remove from the oven and let sit for 10 minutes before serving.

DID YOU KNOW . . .

that Paul's nickname around QVC is "The Traveling QVC Ambassador"?

Dave King

6 to 8 servings

Mimi's Famous Corn Pudding

If you talk with Dave, he'll admit he isn't much of a cook, but he does know good food when he tastes it. So he shared a favorite old family recipe with us. It seems his grandmother, Edna Howe, affectionately known as Mimi, made the "world's best" corn pudding, but only for special occasions and holidays. She never shared her recipe, so I helped him out by creating this one that he says comes pretty darned close to Mimi's.

1 can (15¾ ounces) whole-kernel corn, drained
1 can (14¾ ounces) cream-style corn
½ cup heavy cream
2 eggs
¼ cup biscuit baking mix
2 tablespoons sugar
2 tablespoons butter, melted

Preheat the oven to 375°F. Coat an 8-inch square baking dish with nonstick cooking spray. In a large bowl, combine all the ingredients; whisk until well mixed. Pour into the baking dish and bake for 35 to 40 minutes, or until the pudding is set and the top is golden.

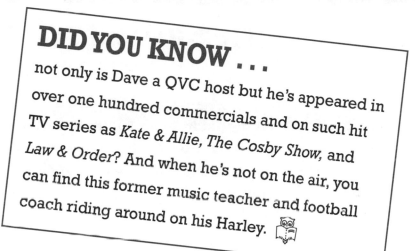

DID YOU KNOW . . .

not only is Dave a QVC host but he's appeared in over one hundred commercials and on such hit TV series as *Kate & Allie, The Cosby Show,* and *Law & Order?* And when he's not on the air, you can find this former music teacher and football coach riding around on his Harley.

Kathy Levine

4 dozen

Black-Bottom Tea Cakes

When I asked Kathy to share a recipe, she gave me a choice between her "killer" kugel and these tea cakes. I tried both and, boy, was it a tough choice! These rich pastries won out by a slim margin with my staff. Now all we need to do is sit down and enjoy them with a cup of hot coffee and Kathy's latest book.

> 1½ cups all-purpose flour
> 1⅓ cups sugar, divided
> ¼ cup unsweetened cocoa
> 1 teaspoon baking soda
> ½ teaspoon plus ⅛ teaspoon salt, divided
> 1 cup water
> ⅓ cup vegetable oil
> 1 teaspoon white vinegar
> 1 teaspoon vanilla extract
> 1 package (8 ounces) cream cheese, softened
> 1 egg
> 1 cup (6 ounces) semisweet chocolate chips

Preheat the oven to 350°F. Coat 48 mini muffin cups with nonstick cooking spray. In a large bowl, combine the flour, 1 cup sugar, the cocoa, baking soda, and ½ teaspoon salt;

mix well. Add the water, oil, vinegar, and vanilla; beat with an electric beater on medium speed for 2 minutes, or until well blended. In a small bowl, combine the cream cheese, egg, and the remaining ⅓ cup sugar and ⅛ teaspoon salt; mix well. Stir in the chocolate chips. Spoon the cocoa batter evenly into the muffin cups, then spoon about 1 teaspoon of the cream cheese mixture into the center of each. Bake for 15 to 18 minutes, or until a wooden toothpick inserted in the center comes out clean. Allow to cool completely. Serve, or cover with plastic wrap.

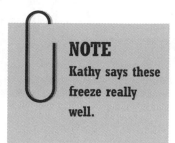

NOTE
Kathy says these freeze really well.

DID YOU KNOW . . .

Kathy was the first host to appear on QVC? She has since accumulated over ten thousand hours of live on-air time. Ask her if she enjoys her time on the air and you know what she'll say? "Mine is the best job in the world!" We can tell how you feel, Kathy, just by watching you!

Ron Maestri

about 1½ quarts

Garden-Fresh Salsa

I asked Ron what his favorite food is and this was his answer: "I am one of those people who could survive on Mexican food. I love anything spicy, and I was always searching for the best salsa in a jar at the supermarket. Since I'd grown tired of trial and error with regard to those store-bought salsas, one day I decided to do it myself. I never saw this recipe anywhere, never read it anywhere. On the spot, I bought all the ingredients I like in a salsa. After the first attempt, it came out perfect! So I'd like to share it with you."

4 large ripe tomatoes, diced
1 large onion, diced
1 bunch fresh cilantro, finely chopped (about 1¼ cups)
¼ cup fresh lemon juice
½ cup red wine vinegar
⅓ cup olive oil
1 teaspoon salt
½ teaspoon black pepper

So-Colorful Fruit Tart

Quic
Apple Cris

B

"AM Style®"
French Toast Loaf

Joan Rivers' Toast

"Weekend Brunch" Scallion "Egg Roll"

Diner Corned Beef Hash

Tova Borgnine's
Scandinavian Gravlax

D

NOTE
Of course this is good served with tortilla chips, but you can also use it to perk up many of your favorite foods.

In a medium glass bowl, combine all the ingredients; mix well. Cover and chill for at least 2 hours before serving.

DID YOU KNOW . . .
Ron has hosted shows on the USA Network and The Travel Channel and his wit has earned him appearances at The Improv, The Comedy Store, The Laugh Factory, and Ice House, to name a few?

Lisa Mason

6 to 8 servings

Vegetable Lasagna

Lisa loves Italian food, and vegetable lasagna is her absolute favorite. She says it's a great dish to have on hand 'cause she can just go home and heat up steaming plates of it for dinner with husband Gino. It's a comforting, hearty, and healthy one-dish meal, perfect for Lisa's busy schedule. (Grab a fork and check it out on color page L.)

9 lasagna noodles
2 tablespoons vegetable oil
2 yellow squash, cut into ½-inch chunks
1 medium zucchini, cut into ½-inch chunks
1 large red bell pepper, chopped
½ pound fresh mushrooms, sliced
3 garlic cloves, minced
1 container (15 ounces) ricotta cheese
2 cups (8 ounces) shredded mozzarella cheese, divided
½ cup grated Parmesan cheese
1 egg
½ teaspoon black pepper
1 jar (28 ounces) spaghetti sauce

Preheat the oven to 375°F. Cook the lasagna noodles according to the package directions; drain and set aside.

Coat a 9" × 13" baking dish with nonstick cooking spray. In a large skillet, heat the oil over medium-high heat. Add the yellow squash, zucchini, bell pepper, mushrooms, and garlic and sauté for 4 to 5 minutes, or until tender. Remove from the heat and set aside. In a large bowl, combine the ricotta cheese, 1½ cups mozzarella cheese, the Parmesan cheese, egg, and black pepper; mix well. Spread one third of the spaghetti sauce evenly over the bottom of the baking dish. Place 3 noodles over the sauce, then spread one third of the cheese mixture over the noodles. Spoon one third of the vegetable mixture over that. Repeat the layers two more times; top with the remaining ½ cup mozzarella cheese. Cover with aluminum foil and bake for 45 minutes. Remove the aluminum foil and bake for 10 to 12 minutes longer, or until heated through and the cheese is golden. Allow to sit for 5 to 10 minutes before serving.

DID YOU KNOW ...

Lisa was honored with the Outstanding Person Award from the Mayor of Oklahoma City for her work with senior citizens and handicapped persons? She also received an Emmy® Award for her documentary *Faces of AIDS.* Good going, Lisa!

Gwen Owens

about 5 dozen

Potato Chip Cookies

These are a longtime favorite of Gwen's family. "They've brightened many recuperating loved ones, many bereaved family members and friends, and even brought cheer to brides-to-be, mothers-to-be, and lots of famished men and women looking for these addicting delights at cookouts, holiday dinners, and parties." Many of her friends have asked for the recipe, but only a few have ever been able to convince her family to divulge the ingredients . . . until now. From Gwen's family to yours, ENJOY!

2 cups (4 sticks) butter, softened
1 cup granulated sugar
3¼ cups all-purpose flour
1 teaspoon vanilla extract
1½ cups coarsely crushed potato chips
¼ cup confectioners' sugar

Preheat the oven to 300°F. In a large bowl, with an electric beater on medium speed, cream the butter and granulated sugar. Slowly blend in the flour and vanilla. Add the crushed potato chips; mix well. Drop by rounded teaspoonfuls 2 inches apart onto ungreased cookie sheets. Using a fork, flatten each cookie. Bake for 18 to 20 minutes, or until light brown around the edges. Remove to a wire rack to cool, then sprinkle with the confectioners' sugar. Serve immediately, or store in an airtight container until ready to serve.

DID YOU KNOW . . .

Gwen has over ten years of TV news experience?
And even though she's now a busy mom of two
daughters, she still has time to dabble in poetry.

Kimberly Parrish

9 to 12 servings

Sweet Potato Casserole

Kim's Grandfather Parrish, who lived to be 101 years old, enjoyed many a Sunday dinner at Kim's house, entertaining the family with stories from days gone by. He especially loved her mom's sweet potato casserole and iced tea, so, according to Kim, his secret to long life was a sweet tooth, a sense of humor, and good family values.

2½ pounds (about 4 medium) sweet potatoes, peeled and cut into 2-inch chunks
1 cup granulated sugar
½ cup plus 3 tablespoons butter, melted, divided
2 eggs, beaten
⅓ cup milk
1 teaspoon vanilla extract
½ cup firmly packed light brown sugar
¼ cup all-purpose flour
½ cup chopped pecans

Place the sweet potato chunks in a soup pot of lightly salted water and boil until tender; drain and place in a large bowl. Preheat the oven to 350°F. Coat a 9" × 13" baking dish with nonstick cooking spray. Mash the potatoes with a potato masher or an electric beater; add the granulated sugar, ½ cup butter, the eggs, milk, and vanilla. Mix well and pour the mixture into the baking dish. In a medium bowl, combine the brown sugar, flour, pecans, and the remaining 3 tablespoons butter; mix until crumbly. Sprinkle over the potatoes and bake for 30 to 35 minutes, or until heated through and bubbly.

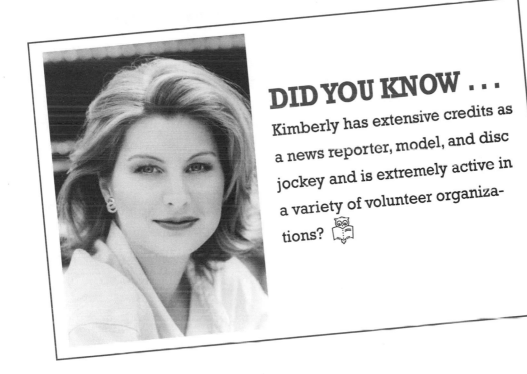

DID YOU KNOW . . .

Kimberly has extensive credits as a news reporter, model, and disc jockey and is extremely active in a variety of volunteer organizations?

Lisa Robertson

6 servings

Dinner Parfaits with Cream Cheese Sauce

When Lisa shared her recipe, here's what else she shared: "I grew up in a rather unusual town, in that everyone was vegetarian. As a result, all my favorite recipes that my mother made when I was growing up were meatless. I know a lot of people think that if you grew up eating meat you could never really like something made with a meat substitute, but everyone we have had over for Sabbath dinner has loved this dish, meat substitute and all! I must admit, it is my favorite of the long list of great meatless dishes my mom made for us growing up."

NOTE
FriChick®, a soy-based chicken substitute made by Worthington, can usually be found in the health food section of the supermarket or at health food stores. Lisa says she'll be surprised if you don't like it.

1 can (12½ ounces) FriChick®, liquid reserved, chopped (see Note)

1 can (10¾ ounces) condensed cream of mushroom soup

1 package (8 ounces) cream cheese, softened

1 can (4 ounces) mushroom pieces, drained

6 scallions (green onions), diced

¼ to ½ of a medium green bell pepper, diced

1 tablespoon chopped pimientos, drained

1 package (10 ounces) Pepperidge Farm Puff Pastry Shells®, baked according to the package directions

In a large saucepan, bring the FriChick® and its liquid, the soup, cream cheese, mushroom pieces, scallions, and green pepper to a boil over medium heat, stirring frequently. Remove from the heat and, just before serving, add the pimientos; mix well. Spoon the mixture into the pastry shells, allowing it to overflow. Serve immediately. (Here's how Lisa serves it: She uses a serving bowl with a larger plate under it and places the filling in the bowl and the pastry shells around the edge of the plate. Then she makes parfaits by serving each person a pastry shell and filling it to overflowing with the FriChick mixture.)

DID YOU KNOW . . .
Lisa's a real science fiction fan? You'd know it if you've seen her hosting the QVC *Star Trek* and *Star Wars* programs!

Mary Beth Roe

12 to 15 servings

Any-Occasion Coffee Cake

Mary Beth is no stranger to the kitchen, either at home or at QVC. When I asked her to share a recipe, she went to her personal recipe collection and pulled out this one. Just as its name says, Mary Beth's coffee cake truly does fit any occasion. We can enjoy it for brunch, dessert, or an any-time snack. It's really versatile, and once it's drizzled with the glaze, it's unforgettable, too!

4 eggs
2 cups granulated sugar
1 cup (2 sticks) butter, softened
1 teaspoon vanilla extract
1 tablespoon baking powder
1 teaspoon salt
3 cups all-purpose flour
1 cup milk
1 cup firmly packed light brown sugar
½ cup chopped walnuts or pecans
2 teaspoons ground cinnamon

Preheat the oven to 325°F. Coat a 9" × 13" baking dish with nonstick cooking spray. In a large bowl, with an electric beater on medium speed, beat the eggs, granulated sugar, butter, vanilla, baking powder, and salt until smooth. Add the flour and milk and beat for 3 to 4 minutes, or until well mixed. Pour half of the batter into the baking dish. In a small bowl, combine the brown sugar, nuts, and cinnamon; mix well. Sprinkle half of the brown sugar mixture evenly over the batter in the baking dish. Pour the remaining batter over that, then sprinkle the top with the remaining brown sugar mixture. Bake for 55 to 60 minutes, or until a wooden toothpick inserted in the center comes out clean. Cut into squares and serve warm, or allow to cool completely before serving.

DID YOU KNOW . . .

Mary Beth considers her family to be her biggest fans? And she says that her rapport with her QVC viewers mirrors the closeness she shares with her family.

Jane Rudolph Treacy

3 to 4 servings

Rudy's Ribs

Jane told me that her father makes some of the most incredible Italian suppers! The one dish that disappears almost instantly at their house is his baby back ribs slow-cooked in spaghetti sauce. They're as interesting and vibrant as their creator and his daughter, and a perfect family recipe for *every* family. (See the tempting photo on color page E.)

Although Jane loves my Death by Chocolate, her true love is husband Sean.

3 to 4 pounds baby back ribs
1 jar (28 ounces) spaghetti sauce
4 fresh basil leaves
1 tablespoon minced garlic
1 teaspoon sugar
1 teaspoon salt
½ teaspoon black pepper

In a large skillet, brown the ribs in batches over medium heat for 5 to 6 minutes per batch. Cut into individual ribs and place in a 3½-quart (or larger) slow cooker. In a medium bowl, combine the remaining ingredients; mix well and pour over the ribs. Cover and cook on the low setting for 7 to 8 hours, or until the ribs are cooked through and tender.

DID YOU KNOW . . .

being a working mom keeps Jane hopping? But in her precious spare time she enjoys traveling, snorkeling, knitting, and skiing. She's also on the board of the American Cancer Society.

Suzanne Runyan

6 to 8 servings

Grandma's Homemade Chicken Noodle Soup

One of Suzanne's fondest childhood memories is of her grandma's chicken noodle soup. The noodles were homemade and Grandma put oodles of them in all her soups, which were also filled with TLC. So get ready to add your own TLC as you carry on her tasty tradition.

NOTE
As long as you're chopping fresh parsley, why not chop a bit extra for sprinkling on top of the soup just before serving?

1½ pounds boneless, skinless chicken breasts, cut into 1-inch chunks

6 cups water

1 can (10½ ounces) condensed chicken broth

2 large carrots, cut into ½-inch slices

2 celery stalks, cut into 2-inch slices

1 small onion, chopped

2 tablespoons chopped fresh parsley (see Note)

½ teaspoon black pepper

1 cup all-purpose flour

1 egg

2 tablespoons milk

½ teaspoon salt

2 tablespoons butter

In a soup pot, combine the chicken, water, broth, carrots, celery, onion, parsley, and pepper; mix well. Bring to a boil over medium heat; cover and cook for 30 minutes. Meanwhile, in a small bowl, combine the flour, egg, milk, and salt; mix well. On a lightly floured surface, with a rolling pin, roll the dough out to form a 10" × 12" rectangle. Cut into ¼" × 5" strips. Allow the noodles to sit for 15 minutes, then drop a few at a time into the soup. Cook, uncovered, for 15 minutes, or until the noodles and vegetables are tender. Stir in the butter until melted, then serve.

DID YOU KNOW . . .

Suzanne is as comfortable behind the camera as she is in front of it? That's 'cause she's worked as a freelance news photographer, and her work has appeared in many places, including *ABC World News Tonight*.

Lynne Tucker

6 to 8 servings

Summer Pasta

This summer pasta is a longtime favorite of Lynne's—and a new favorite of mine, 'cause it's light but still packed with great taste. And don't let the name fool you—summer pasta is perfect all year-round, especially for afternoon get-togethers and light evening meals.

4 medium ripe tomatoes, cut into 1-inch chunks (see Note)
½ medium red onion, thinly sliced
¾ cup red wine vinegar
¼ cup olive oil
2 garlic cloves, minced
½ cup chopped fresh basil
2 tablespoons chopped fresh dill
1 pound linguine, spaghetti, or your favorite pasta (see Note)
¼ cup (½ stick) butter, softened
½ cup grated Parmesan or Romano cheese

NOTE
Lynne suggests blanching the tomatoes in boiling water for a few seconds before chopping them so the skins will slide off. Sometimes she makes this recipe with bow tie pasta, chills the entire combination, and serves it as a pasta salad dish. Feel free to top it with fresh ground pepper and additional grated Parmesan or Romano cheese, if you'd like.

In a large bowl, combine the tomatoes, onion, vinegar, oil, garlic, basil, and dill; mix well. Cover and chill for 30 minutes. In a soup pot, cook the pasta according to the package directions; drain. Return to the pot and add the butter and cheese; toss until the butter is melted and the pasta is well coated. Serve the pasta with the chilled tomato mixture on top for a hot pasta/chilled topping combination that makes this recipe unique.

DID YOU KNOW ...

Lynne owned an Italian restaurant in Santa Monica, California? Yup, she served up lots of tasty pasta dishes, just like this one!

David Venable

6 to 8 servings

Baked Corn Casserole

David and I are longtime friends from his days anchoring the news on WTAJ-TV, where my show aired in Altoona, Pennsylvania. That's what he was up to in the days when he created this recipe. It's a casserole that's perfect for any holiday or special occasion meal 'cause it's so easy and so tasty. (See how tempting it looks on color page E.)

DID YOU KNOW . . .

as part of David's duties as a QVC host, he has toured Italian gold factories and has visited Brazil, Ireland, Germany, and England for product research? It's not hard to see why David loves his job!

1 package (8½ ounces) corn muffin mix
1 can (15¾ ounces) whole-kernel corn, drained
1 can (14¾ ounces) cream-style corn
1 cup sour cream
½ cup (1 stick) butter, softened
1 egg

NOTE
David suggests adding a chopped red bell pepper for a burst of color.

Preheat the oven to 350°F. In a large bowl, combine all the ingredients; mix well. Pour into a 2-quart casserole dish. Cover and bake for 30 minutes. Uncover and bake for 30 to 35 more minutes, or until set and the top is golden.

Dan Wheeler

9 to 12 squares

Frozen Rice Krispies Treats®

Dan not only shares his love of sports with QVC viewers but with his family, too.

Here's a recipe that Dan's mom, Marge, used to make for him when he was a kid. It was kind of a reward when he did something right—like getting through a French class without having to stand in the corner for talking too much (in English). (Watching Dan on QVC today, you can probably tell that he still loves to talk!) He looks forward to these treats to this day, and Dan wants to thank his mom for being his hero.

1 cup Rice Krispies® cereal
½ cup chopped walnuts
½ cup sweetened flaked coconut
½ cup firmly packed light brown sugar
½ cup (1 stick) butter, melted
1 quart vanilla ice cream, softened

In a large bowl, combine all the ingredients except the ice cream; mix well. Spoon half of the mixture over the bottom of an 8-inch square baking dish. Spread the ice cream over the top, then top with the remaining cereal mixture. Cover and freeze for at least 4 hours, or until firm. Cut into squares and serve; cover and store any remaining squares in the freezer.

DID YOU KNOW ...

that Dan's a self-proclaimed sports nut? He loves working as a QVC program host 'cause it gives him the opportunity to meet many of his sports idols.

Leah Williams

8 enchiladas

Chicken Enchiladas

Since Leah is a native of California, Mexican food is her absolute favorite. She especially enjoys chicken enchiladas, so she shared this speedy and tasty recipe that she makes for her friends. I'm so glad she includes me in that lucky group!

1 can (10¾ ounces) condensed cream of chicken soup
½ cup sour cream
½ cup (2 ounces) shredded Monterey Jack cheese
½ cup (2 ounces) shredded Cheddar cheese
¼ cup (1 ounce) shredded pepper-Jack cheese
2 tablespoons butter
1 small onion, chopped
1 teaspoon chili powder
2 cups diced cooked chicken
1 jar (4.25 ounces) chopped jalapeño peppers, drained (see Note)
Eight 8-inch flour tortillas

Preheat the oven to 375°F. Coat a 9" × 13" baking dish with nonstick cooking spray. In a small bowl, combine the soup and sour cream; mix well and set aside. In a medium bowl, combine the 3 cheeses; mix well and set aside. Melt the butter in a large saucepan over medium heat. Add the onion and chili powder and sauté for 2 to 3 minutes, or until the onion is tender. Stir in the chicken, jalapeño peppers, 2 tablespoons of the soup mixture, and ¼ cup of the cheese mixture. Cook for 2 to 3 minutes, or until heated through and the cheese has melted. Spoon the chicken mixture down the centers of the tortillas. Roll the tortillas tightly and place seam side down in the baking dish. Pour the remaining soup mixture evenly over the top. Cover with aluminum foil and bake for 15 minutes. Uncover and sprinkle the remaining cheese mixture over the top. Bake for 5 to 8 minutes, or until heated through and the cheese has melted.

> **NOTE**
> It's nice to dress this up with a sprinkle of chopped parsley or cilantro just before serving. And remember, the jalapeño peppers make it spicy, so if you prefer a less spicy dish, use a can of chopped mild green chilies in place of them.

DID YOU KNOW . . .

Leah's motto is "Go for your dream, because it can happen"? After flying across the country for her QVC audition, she was offered her dream job as Program Host.

Guest Appearances

Besides all the hosts, there are many guests who visit QVC's studio on a regular basis. Sharing everything from makeup and jewelry to kitchen gadgets, exercise videos, and works of art, these are people I run into from time to time in the Green Room before and after my segments. So I asked a bunch of them to be part of this book, and I'm thrilled that they were gracious enough to add their unique and tasty recipes to our QVC collection.

Guest Appearances

Denise Austin

6 servings

Pork and Grapefruit Stir-Fry

We've all seen Denise Austin's exercise videos and equipment on QVC and learned it's not just what you eat, but how you live, too. Exercise is important to Denise . . . and so is grapefruit, 'cause it's a tasty source of Vitamin C (and it's fat-free, too)! She loves to mix it into new recipes and this one's a scrumptious change from everyday stir-fry combinations.

NOTE
To make slicing the pork loin really easy, place it in the freezer for a few hours to freeze slightly, then slice. And I like to make it just a bit sweeter by adding ¼ cup honey.

1 cup Ruby Red Florida grapefruit juice

3 tablespoons light soy sauce

2 tablespoons cornstarch

1 tablespoon honey (see Note)

½ teaspoon ground ginger

1 tablespoon vegetable oil

3 medium zucchini, thinly sliced

1 medium red bell pepper, cut into ½-inch strips

1½ pounds boneless pork loin, trimmed and thinly sliced (see Note)

1 tablespoon sesame seeds, toasted

In a large bowl, combine the grapefruit juice, soy sauce, cornstarch, honey, and ginger; mix well and set aside. In a large skillet, heat the oil over medium-high heat. Add the zucchini and bell pepper and stir-fry for 2 to 3 minutes, or

62

until crisp-tender. Remove the vegetables and set aside. Stir-fry half of the pork for 2 to 3 minutes, or until no pink remains; remove from the skillet and repeat with the other half of the pork. Return all the pork and vegetables to the skillet and add the grapefruit juice mixture; mix well. Cook for 2 to 3 minutes, or until thickened and bubbly, stirring constantly. Sprinkle the sesame seeds over the top and serve.

DID YOU KNOW . . .

in addition to her series of books and videos, Denise has her own exercise show, *Daily Workout*, on the Lifetime network?

Despite a busy work schedule, Denise always "works out" time to spend with her family.

Tova Borgnine

about 2 pounds

Scandinavian Gravlax

When it comes to making us look good, Tova Borgnine is a star. But when I asked Tova to share a recipe with me, she said, "I can't cook." I said, "C'mon, everyone has at least one recipe." Her reply? "The only time I did attempt to create a sumptuous meal for my beloved husband, I ended up in the emergency room of a local hospital. Since then I refer to our kitchen as 'the other room.'" If you want to know more about that incident, and others like it, you'll have to read Tova's book, *Being Married Happily Forever*. You know, she finally did admit to liking gravlax, which is similar to smoked salmon, popular in her native Norway, and she happily shared her mother's recipe. (See how elegant it looks on color page D.)

½ cup firmly packed dark brown sugar

¼ cup black peppercorns, crushed

½ cup kosher (coarse) salt

¼ cup finely chopped fresh chives

2 tablespoons finely chopped fresh dill

Two 1-pound fresh salmon fillets, skin left on

½ cup aquavit or tequila (see Note)

¼ cup finely chopped fresh cilantro

One 16-inch square cheesecloth

64

In a small bowl, combine the brown sugar, crushed pepper-corns, and salt; mix well. In another small bowl, combine the chives and dill; mix well. Place the cheesecloth on a flat surface. Place 1 salmon fillet skin side down in the center of the cheesecloth. Spread the brown sugar mixture evenly over the top; sprinkle with the chive mixture, then with the aquavit. When the aquavit has been absorbed, place the remaining salmon fillet skin side up on top. Wrap the cheesecloth around the salmon, pulling the cloth as tightly as possible. Place on a wire rack on a rimmed baking sheet. Place another baking sheet on top of the salmon mixture, then top with a 5-pound weight. Allow to cure in the refrigerator for 3 days, turning every 24 hours; liquid will be pressed out and will accumulate on the baking sheet. Remove the cheesecloth and discard. Using a knife, scrape the herbs off the salmon, then rinse with cold water and pat dry with paper towels. Cover the flesh side of the salmon with the chopped cilantro. Using a sharp knife, slice as thinly as possible at a 45-degree angle, making green-edged ribbons of gravlax.

NOTE
Aquavit is a clear, Scandinavian liquor flavored with caraway seeds. Serve the gravlax on small slices of pumpernickel bread with dill mustard sauce and wedges of lemon.

Photograph by Gordon Munro

DID YOU KNOW . . .
Tova's husband is the famous television and movie actor Ernest Borgnine?

George Foreman

4 servings

Grilled Tarragon Chicken

Photograph by Charles Schabes of Charles Schabes Photography, Chicago, IL

George has been known to pack quite a punch—and that goes for his recipes, too, like this grilled chicken that's packed with loads of juicy flavor. If you don't have his dynamite Lean Mean Fat-Reducing Grilling Machine yet, you'd better hurry and get one . . . 'cause we wouldn't want to upset George.

4 boneless, skinless chicken breast halves (1 to 1½ pounds total)

½ cup olive oil

2 tablespoons chopped fresh parsley

1 teaspoon dried tarragon

1 teaspoon salt

½ teaspoon black pepper

Place each chicken breast between two sheets of plastic wrap. Using a mallet, pound to a ¼-inch thickness. In a large bowl, combine the remaining ingredients; mix well. Add the chicken to the seasoning mixture, turning to coat

66

well on both sides. Cover and marinate in the refrigerator for at least 2 hours. Preheat the grilling machine for 5 minutes (see Note). Grill the chicken for 4 to 5 minutes, or until no pink remains.

NOTE
George's grilling machine works like magic, but if you haven't gotten yours yet, this chicken can also be cooked on a barbecue grill or an indoor grill pan for 4 to 5 minutes per side, or until no pink remains.

DID YOU KNOW . . .

George has five sons . . . all named George?!

Naomi Judd

4 servings

Naomi's Favorite Bus Meal

So, how did Naomi manage to cook meals while spending so much time on the road? Well, when I asked her, this is what she told me: "A wok and a slow cooker come in handy if you ever travel on a bus or in a camper, or live in a small apartment. This stir-fry dish is good with any of your favorite steamed fresh vegetables, such as broccoli, spinach, green beans, or zucchini. There's just 2 ounces of meat per serving in this dish, but often I omit the meat and just do the veggies and serve them over brown rice with soy sauce."

Cover photograph by Chip Powell

DID YOU KNOW . . .

with her daughter, singing sensation Wynonna, Naomi was part of one of country's hottest singing duos, the Judds?

2 tablespoons peanut oil, or more as needed

½ pound flank steak, thinly sliced across the grain

2 medium carrots, trimmed and thinly sliced

1 cup broccoli pieces (optional)

1 cup green beans, in pieces (optional)

1 can (8 ounces) sliced water chestnuts, drained

2 cups sliced fresh mushrooms

1 medium onion, chopped

1 tablespoon minced fresh ginger

1 cup snow peas, strings removed

2 tablespoons soy sauce

4 ounces fresh spinach leaves (5 cups tightly packed),
    washed and tough stems removed

2 cups cooked brown rice

In a large wok or nonstick skillet, heat the 2 tablespoons oil over medium-high heat. Add the meat and stir-fry until no longer pink, about 1 minute. Remove the meat. Add the carrots, broccoli, and green beans, if using, water chestnuts, mushrooms, onion, and ginger, and more oil if needed. Stir-fry until crisp-tender, about 3 minutes. Return the meat to the wok and stir in the snow peas and soy sauce. Cover with the spinach leaves, then cover the wok and heat through until the spinach is wilted, 1 to 2 minutes. Serve over brown rice.

Thomas Kinkade

4 to 6 servings

El Dorado Beef Casserole

If you've ever seen Thomas Kinkade on QVC, you know how amazing he is and that his paintings are incredible. Well, he's no slouch in the kitchen, either! Thom, who grew up in California's El Dorado County, said that every year on his birthday he gave his mom the same answer when she asked what he wanted her to make him for his birthday dinner. He always wanted her beef casserole. She must have been pretty creative herself . . . just try this tasty dish and see for yourself. We should all be thankful that Thom shared the recipe so that each of us can enjoy it on our own birthday . . . or any day, for that matter.

½ pound ground beef
1 medium onion, chopped
2 cans (8 ounces each) tomato sauce
1 cup water
¼ teaspoon chili powder
1 package (9 ounces) tortilla chips, coarsely crushed
1 cup sour cream
1 cup (4 ounces) shredded Monterey Jack cheese

Preheat the oven to 375°F. Coat a 1½-quart casserole dish with nonstick cooking spray. In a large skillet, brown the ground beef and onion over medium-high heat for 5 minutes. Add the tomato sauce, water, and chili powder; mix well. Reduce the heat to medium-low and simmer for 2 to 3 minutes, or until thickened. Spread one third of the beef mixture in the casserole dish, then top with one third of the crushed tortilla chips, one third of the sour cream, and one third of the cheese. Repeat the layers two more times, ending with cheese. Bake for 25 to 30 minutes, or until bubbly and the top is golden.

DID YOU KNOW . . .

Thom is known as "The Painter of Light"? His works are known for such dramatic effects as glowing windows, reflected images, and pictorial lighting.

6 to 8 servings

Bob Mackie

Roasted Peppers

Since so many of us have picked up spectacular fashions by Bob Mackie on QVC, we know he's a whiz with a pencil and sketch pad. But guess what?! He's a kitchen whiz, too, and these flavorful roasted peppers are proof! Try them alone or as a side to any sandwich. And teamed with Tova Borgnine's Scandinavian Gravlax (color page D), you've got a sure winner every time!

> 6 bell peppers (2 red, 2 yellow, and 2 green), quartered
> 1 can (2 ounces) flat anchovies in oil, drained
> 3 tablespoons skim milk
> 6 tablespoons extra virgin olive oil
> 3 tablespoons white wine vinegar
> ¼ teaspoon salt
> ¼ teaspoon black pepper

Preheat the broiler. Line a large rimmed baking sheet with aluminum foil. Place the bell peppers skin side up on the baking sheet and broil for 8 to 10 minutes, or until the skins have blackened. Immediately place in a large resealable plastic storage bag and set aside. When almost cool, remove the peppers from the bag and carefully peel off the skin without tearing the pulp; place the slices on a serving platter. In a small bowl, cover the anchovies with milk and allow to soak for 5 minutes; drain and pat dry with paper towels. Arrange the anchovies in a basket-weave pattern over the roasted peppers (see photo, color page D). In a small bowl, whisk together the remaining ingredients until well combined. Drizzle over the roasted peppers and anchovies and serve.

DID YOU KNOW . . .

Bob has designed costumes for TV, films, and Broadway for three decades? His extraordinary work was widely seen on *The Carol Burnett Show* for eleven years and Bob continues to design unique fashions for today's most visible celebrities.

Joy Mangano

12 to 16 servings

Joy's Creamy-Delicious Cheesecake

Joy Mangano is famous for inventing the Miracle Mop®, and now she's come up with another terrific product: the Piatto™ Bakery Box. She had to! Joy says that's because she always loved baking this cheesecake for her family and friends, but whenever she took it somewhere it would end up crushed. So now we can all have the perfect dessert carrier . . . and her creamy cheesecake recipe, too!

11 cinnamon graham crackers (1 sleeve), crushed
1 tablespoon butter, melted
1 tablespoon water
3 packages (8 ounces each) cream cheese, softened
1¼ cups sugar
4 eggs
1½ teaspoons vanilla extract
1 container (16 ounces) sour cream
1 cup heavy cream

Preheat the oven to 350°F. Coat a 10-inch springform pan with nonstick cooking spray. In a medium bowl, combine the graham cracker crumbs, butter, and water; mix well. Press into the springform pan, covering the bottom to form a crust. In a large bowl, with an electric beater on medium speed, beat the cream cheese, sugar, 1 egg, and the vanilla until creamy. Add the remaining eggs and beat until thoroughly combined. Add the sour cream and heavy cream and beat until creamy. Pour into the crust and bake for 35 to 40 minutes, or until firm around the edges. Turn off the oven and open the door for 1 minute, then close the door and let the cake sit in the oven for 15 minutes. Remove from the oven and allow to cool, then cover and chill for 6 to 8 hours.

DID YOU KNOW . . .

Joy invented the Miracle Mop® as a way of cleaning the teak deck of her sailboat? It's different from traditional mops because it won't scratch as it cleans!

about 1½ pounds

Suze Orman

Dollar-Wise and Pound-Foolish Toffee

With all of Suze Orman's money-saving hints and especially her advice on how to stretch our dollars, she's become a popular QVC guest. Know what? She's popular in the kitchen, too. When she shared this recipe, she said it's dollar-wise, meaning it won't hurt our wallets to make it, but it's pound-foolish, 'cause it may widen our waistlines a little more than we'd like!

> ### NOTE
> To test for the hard crack stage: Drop a bit of the mixture from a teaspoon into a glass of cold water. If it forms a ball that hardens in the water, then it has reached the hard crack stage. If not, continue to cook the mixture, then test it again after a bit.

1 cup (2 sticks) butter
1 cup sugar
¼ cup light corn syrup
1 cup pecans, finely chopped, divided
1 teaspoon vanilla extract
1½ cups milk chocolate chips

Coat a 10" × 15" rimmed baking sheet with nonstick cooking spray. In a soup pot, combine the butter, sugar, and corn syrup. Bring to a boil over medium-high heat and boil for 3 to 4 minutes, until the mixture reaches the hard crack stage (see Note), stirring constantly. Remove from the heat and stir in ½ cup pecans and the vanilla; quickly spread over the baking sheet. Sprinkle the chocolate chips evenly over the mixture and allow to melt, then use a knife to spread the melted chocolate over the toffee, covering it completely. Sprinkle the remaining ½ cup pecans over the melted chocolate and chill for at least 1 hour, or until the chocolate is firm. Break into bite-sized pieces and serve, or store in an airtight container until ready to serve.

Photograph by Kelly Campbell

DID YOU KNOW . . .

Suze Orman's book, *The 9 Steps to Financial Freedom*, was a national bestseller and a one-hour PBS television special based on this title ran in early 1998? Suze also keeps busy writing a regular financial column for *Self* magazine and recently edited and contributed to a financial magazine supplement called *Currency* for Condé Nast.

Victoria Principal

2 to 4 servings

Secret Cheese-Stuffed Trout

Photograph by Jeff Katz

Victoria became well known for her long-time role on the popular TV show *Dallas*, but since then she's gained recognition as a successful businesswoman, too. She has worked with a team of experts to develop a revolutionary skin care system, which she brings to QVC often. Since she believes that looking and feeling good begin with eating right, Victoria shared this scrumptious trout recipe with us. Who'd know that she modified it slightly for those of us watching our figures? It'll be our secret! Serve this to guests and you'll even impress yourself.

½ cup sliced fresh mushrooms
¼ cup chopped scallions
2 tablespoons grated Parmesan cheese
2 whole trout (1 pound each), cleaned, rinsed, and dried
⅛ teaspoon black pepper

Preheat the broiler. Line a rimmed baking sheet with aluminum foil and coat with nonstick cooking spray. In a medium bowl, combine the mushrooms, scallions, and cheese; mix well. Spoon evenly into the cavities of the trout and secure with wooden toothpicks or skewers. Season the outside of the trout with the pepper and place on the baking sheet. Broil 4 to 5 inches from the heat for 8 to 10 minutes per side, or until the fish flakes easily with a fork. Remove the toothpicks and serve immediately.

DID YOU KNOW . . .

in addition to her skin care line, Victoria heads up Victoria Principal Productions, for which she develops, produces, and stars in numerous television projects?

Chef Paul Prudhomme

4 servings

Sautéed Scallops

Like me, Paul grew up in a family that loved food and cooking. He learned most of his secrets right in the heart of Louisiana, and now uses them in his New Orleans restaurant. So here's a yummy recipe from Paul that uses his own blend of spices to make it extra special.

NOTE

Paul offers this "lagniappe," which means "a little something extra," with his recipe: Shaking the pan in a back-and-forth motion and the continuous release of water from the scallops into the melting butter keeps the sauce from separating and having an oily texture. Stirring doesn't produce the same effect.

¼ pound (1 stick) plus 2 tablespoons unsalted butter or margarine
2 tablespoons Chef Paul Prudhomme's Seafood Magic®
1½ pounds scallops (3½ cups)
½ cup finely chopped scallions (green onions)
2 tablespoons finely chopped parsley leaves
2 cups sliced fresh mushrooms

Melt half the butter in a large skillet (preferably not a non-stick type) over high heat. Add the Seafood Magic and cook for about 10 seconds, stirring once or twice. Add the scallops, scallions, and parsley, stirring well. Cook about 1 minute, stirring once or twice. Add the remaining butter and the mushrooms. Cook for about 3 minutes, constantly shaking the pan fairly vigorously in a back-and-forth motion. (After 2 minutes, stir, so the mushrooms get coated.) Remove from the heat and serve immediately over rice, tossed with pasta, or in a bowl with lots of warm French bread on the side.

DID YOU KNOW . . .

K-Paul's Louisiana Kitchen, Chef Paul's New Orleans restaurant, has been named one of the top ten in the country? And when we can't travel to "The Big Easy," we can still enjoy those great flavors with Paul's own line of seasoning blends, hot sauce, and other food products, available, of course, from QVC.

Joan Rivers

2 pieces of toast

Joan Rivers' Toast

Joan Rivers is a pro in the fashion and jewelry departments, but when it comes to the kitchen, she sometimes needs a little extra help. She tells me she's not much of a cook, but she does have one recipe that's been in her family for generations. Over the years, she's perfected it and now she has shared it with all of us.

2 slices white bread (see Note)
2 pats butter or margarine

Says Joan: "Take two slices of white bread. Place them in a toaster and press down the handle. Wait for 2 minutes, or until the toast pops up. Spread a pat of butter or margarine over each slice *after* removing it from the toaster."

DID YOU KNOW . . .

besides Joan's QVC jewelry appearances, she covers the Oscar® Awards pre-show and many other award pre-shows and fashion reviews for E! Television, and even has her own radio show?

Backstage Bits

Over the years, my QVC backstage friends have always told me how much they enjoy my visits. I used to think it was because of my witty personality and charm. But lately I've started thinking it has something to do with all the food I bring with me. After all, they don't call me Mr. Food for nothing!

Whenever I'm at QVC, I make sure to take extra-special care of the backstage crew. Sometimes they get to sample dishes made from recipes in my books, while other times I make little treats especially for them. After I finish my show, I'll mix a little of this with a little of that and usually end up with a darned good recipe . . . without any fuss! So here are some of my all-time best backstage concoctions. Why, it's as if you're getting a special backstage pass to your own feeding frenzy!

Backstage Bits

Eye-Opening Burritos

4 servings

I can still remember the day my Tex-Mex cookbook debuted. It was early in the morning and it seemed like everybody backstage was starving. Since I'm such a big breakfast person, I decided to whip up breakfast after my show. Hmm, what ingredients did I have besides eggs? Leftover tortillas, a little bit of Mexican cheese, and some chilies. The result? Eye-opening breakfast burritos that satisfied everybody on the set and are sure to satisfy your hungry gang, too.

8 eggs
1 can (4 ounces) chopped green chilies, drained
3 tablespoons real bacon bits
Four 8-inch flour tortillas
2 cups (8 ounces) shredded Mexican cheese blend
2 tablespoons butter

In a large bowl, combine the eggs, chilies, and bacon bits; whisk until well combined, then set aside. Heat the tortillas one at a time in a large skillet over medium-high heat for 20 to 30 seconds per side, or until heated through. Place the tortillas on a serving platter; place ½ cup cheese down the center of each tortilla and cover to keep warm. Melt the butter in the skillet, then add the egg mixture. Scramble the eggs, cooking until just set. Top each tortilla with one quarter of the scrambled egg mixture. Roll up and serve immediately.

NOTE
You can give these a great look by topping each with sour cream, salsa, and scallion rings. You can also add any of those to the tortillas before rolling them; it makes a quick meal to go!

DID YOU KNOW . . .
burrito is Spanish for "little donkey"? Originally from northern Mexico, burritos traditionally are flour tortillas wrapped around meats, cheeses, or beans.

Throw-Together Chicken Vegetable Soup

8 to 10 servings

DID YOU KNOW . . .

the alias for chicken soup? It's Jewish Penicillin, and it's called that for its mysterious healing powers (Jewish mothers have sworn by it for years)!

Winters are pretty darned cold in the Philadelphia area, where QVC is based. That's why a big pot of steaming soup is always welcomed there. When I was there promoting my Chicken, Pasta, and Dessert book trio, a cold front hit the Northeast and the temperature dropped thirty degrees in minutes. The snow just kept falling, and I actually got snowed in at QVC. So I took some leftover veggies and chicken, tossed 'em in a big pot, and in about fifteen minutes I had a hot and hearty soup. You never saw anything disappear so fast. You could say that my throw-together soup was a real sellout!

10 cups water
10 chicken bouillon cubes
3 cups shredded cooked chicken
1 package (16 ounces) frozen mixed vegetables, thawed
½ teaspoon black pepper

In a soup pot, combine the water and bouillon cubes and bring to a boil over medium-high heat. Boil until the bouillon cubes have dissolved, stirring occasionally. Add the remaining ingredients and return to a boil. Reduce the heat to medium-low and simmer for 10 to 15 minutes, or until the vegetables are tender.

Strawberry-Kiwi Smoothie

4 servings

Unlike the winters, the summers in Philadelphia are pretty hot. Can you think of a better way to cool off than with a refreshing smoothie? Since most of us usually have a little extra fruit on hand in the summer, it takes no time to make this great afternoon pick-me-up and cool-me-down all in one.

½ cup milk
1 pint fresh strawberries, washed and hulled
1 kiwi, peeled and cut into chunks
2 teaspoons sugar (see Note)
1 quart vanilla ice cream

In a blender, blend all the ingredients except the ice cream until the fruit is pureed. Add the ice cream and blend until the mixture is smooth and thick. Serve immediately.

NOTE
Add more or less sugar, depending on the sweetness of the strawberries. For a lighter version, use nonfat frozen yogurt and skim milk.

DID YOU KNOW . . .

that smoothies have been around since the 1970s? Usually a mix of fruit and milk, yogurt, frozen yogurt, or ice cream, they can be made in lots of yummy flavor combinations!

Chocolate-Dipped Cookies

about 4 dozen

NOTE
Feel free to use walnuts, pecans, almonds, hazelnuts, or macadamia nuts—whatever's your favorite.

My split-second cookies have always been a favorite, and I've heard from loads of people who say it's as much fun to make 'em as it is to eat 'em. Well, one day after a show I had a batch of leftover dough and got an idea of how to use it differently. I baked it as drop cookies, then dipped them into a big bowl of melted chocolate and then into some chopped nuts and before I knew it, I had come up with the best chocolate-dipped cookies I'd ever tasted! They look so fancy, yet who would guess how easy they are! And just think, I came upon them by luck. Lucky us!

¾ cup (1½ sticks) butter, softened
⅔ cup sugar
1 egg
2 teaspoons vanilla extract
2 cups all-purpose flour
½ teaspoon baking powder
1 package (12 ounces) semisweet chocolate chips
2 tablespoons vegetable shortening
2½ cups chopped peanuts (see Note)

Preheat the oven to 350°F. In a large bowl, with an electric beater on low speed, beat the butter, sugar, egg, and vanilla until creamy. Add the flour and baking powder and continue beating until well combined. Form into 1-inch balls and place 2 inches apart on ungreased cookie sheets; using your hand, flatten the balls. Bake for 8 to 10 minutes, or until the edges are golden. Remove to a wire rack to cool completely. Line cookie sheets with waxed paper. In a small saucepan, melt the choco-

late and shortening over medium-low heat, stirring constantly. Remove from the heat and dip each cookie halfway into the melted chocolate mixture, then into the chopped peanuts. Place on the cookie sheets and allow the chocolate to harden, chilling if necessary. Serve, or place in an airtight container until ready to serve.

The QVC phone lines are always buzzing . . . and their operators are always cheerful!

DID YOU KNOW . . .

nuts are one of the most versatile foods? They can be used in every part of a meal, from soups and salads to breads, main dishes, and desserts!

Meat Loaf Wellington

6 servings

It was in the fall of 1996 that I presented my *Meat Around the Table* cookbook. And it just happened to be dinnertime, too, so it wasn't hard to find volunteers backstage to help me eat up the leftover meat loaf from my segment, especially since I made it portable by wrapping and baking each piece in leftover puff pastry. What used to be plain meat loaf was suddenly Meat Loaf Wellington. It may sound very fancy, and it sure looks it . . . but it's very easy, too.

2 pounds ground beef
1 cup Italian-flavored bread crumbs
1 cup ketchup, divided
1 large onion, finely chopped
2 eggs
½ teaspoon salt
½ teaspoon black pepper
1 package (17¼ ounces) puff pastry (2 sheets), thawed

Preheat the oven to 375°F. In a medium bowl, combine the ground beef, bread crumbs, ½ cup ketchup, the onion, eggs, salt, and pepper; mix well and place in a 9" × 5" loaf pan. Spread the remaining ½ cup ketchup over the top and bake for 1 to 1¼ hours, or until the juices run clear. Remove from the oven and allow to cool completely; cut the cooled meat loaf into six equal slices. Preheat the oven to 450°F. On a lightly floured surface, with a rolling pin, roll out each sheet of pastry to about a 15-inch square; cut each sheet into three equal strips. Place one slice of meat loaf ½ inch from the top end of each strip of pastry and brush the edges of the pastry with water. Bring the bottom edge of each up to meet the top edge, covering the meat loaf completely. Seal the edges and crimp with a fork. Place the packets on a large rimmed baking sheet and bake for 20 to 25 minutes, or until heated through and the pastry is golden.

NOTE
Serve these with a mushroom gravy spooned over the top of each. And to make preparation even simpler, I usually make the meat loaf the night before I plan to serve it; then it's ready to wrap in the puff pastry just before baking and serving.

DID YOU KNOW . . .

in classic Beef Wellington, fillet of beef is wrapped in a pastry crust along with pâté and sautéed finely chopped mushrooms?

Creamy Ambrosia Trifle

10 to 12 servings

NOTE

I like to reserve some of the cherries, oranges, and coconut to use as a garnish on top of the trifle.

I'm no stranger to trifles, so whenever I have leftover cake, I get ready to put together a new and different version. One night when I had leftover angel food cake, I layered it with some coconut and cut-up fresh fruit that I had on hand. That one came out so good that I wanted to repeat it . . . again and again. Oh, I almost forgot to mention the best part—the layers of custard sauce that hold this trifle together. Mmm, mmm!

1 can (14 ounces) sweetened condensed milk
⅓ cup lemon juice
9 drops yellow food color
One 10-ounce angel food cake, cut into 1-inch chunks
1 jar (10 ounces) maraschino cherries, drained
1 can (11 ounces) mandarin oranges, drained
1½ cups sweetened flaked coconut, toasted
1 container (16 ounces) frozen whipped topping, thawed

DID YOU KNOW . . .

that mandarin oranges can be as small as golf balls and as large as baseballs?!

In a small bowl, combine the sweetened condensed milk, lemon juice, and food color; mix well. In a trifle dish or large glass serving bowl, layer one third of the cake chunks, one third of the cherries, and one third of the oranges; drizzle with one third of the lemon mixture. Sprinkle with one third of the coconut and top with one third of the whipped topping. Repeat the layers two more times, cover, and chill for at least 2 hours before serving.

Barbecued Chicken Pizza

6 to 8 servings

You've probably seen me at the grill outside QVC many times, and when it comes to the barbecue, I guess most of us could say that our eyes are bigger than our stomachs. I always seem to have leftover barbecued chicken, so what better way to use it than on a pizza? That's right, I said pizza. All we do is cut the leftover chicken into chunks, add a little more barbecue sauce, sprinkle it with some corn kernels, and top it with some grated cheese. Here's a recipe for starting it from scratch so you can serve barbecued chicken anytime, rain or shine.

1 tablespoon vegetable oil
1 pound boneless, skinless chicken thighs, cut into ½-inch chunks (see Note)
¾ cup barbecue sauce
One 12-inch prepared pizza shell (see Note)
1 can (11 ounces) Mexican-style corn, drained
1½ cups (6 ounces) shredded Colby-Jack cheese blend

Preheat the oven to 450°F. In a large skillet, heat the oil over medium-high heat. Add the chicken and cook for 5 to 6 minutes, or until no pink remains; drain off the oil from the pan. Add the barbecue sauce; mix well and cook until heated. Place the pizza shell on a pizza pan and spread the chicken mixture evenly over the top. Spread the corn over the chicken mixture, then top with the cheese. Bake for 10 to 12 minutes, or until the cheese is melted and the crust is crisp and brown.

DID YOU KNOW . . .
pizza is one of the most popular snacks and meals in the United States? Today it's found in so many varieties. Its Italian originators wouldn't recognize it!

NOTE
Wanna use leftover chicken like I did at QVC? About 2 cups of cooked chicken chunks will do the trick. We can also use fresh or frozen bread dough spread over the pizza pan, topped as above, and baked for 2 to 3 minutes longer.

93

Shrimp Scampi Salad

4 to 6 servings

Sara Sirchie helps me get wired for sound so that you can hear each and every "Mmm," "Aah," and "OOH IT'S SO GOOD!!®"

The price of shrimp is sure to pinch our pocketbooks these days, so I've come up with a way we can stretch it just a bit: Make it salad style. And this way it combines two favorites in one. You see, it all started backstage when I couldn't decide which way to use leftover shrimp—make it scampi style or top a salad with it and some creamy dressing. So I decided to try both in one dish and now we've got garlicky shrimp scampi combined with a touch of cream and tossed with crispy lettuce. Serve this when you really want to impress the gang.

¼ cup (½ stick) butter

12 garlic cloves, minced

2 tablespoons chopped fresh parsley

1 tablespoon fresh lemon juice

½ teaspoon salt

¼ teaspoon black pepper

1 pound large shrimp, peeled and deveined

½ cup heavy cream

1 medium head romaine lettuce, cut into bite-sized pieces

94

In a large skillet, melt the butter over medium heat. Add the garlic, parsley, lemon juice, salt, and pepper; cook, stirring occasionally, for 2 to 3 minutes, or until the garlic is golden. Add the shrimp and cook for 2 to 3 minutes, or until the shrimp turn pink. Reduce the heat to low and stir in the cream until well combined; remove from the heat. Place the lettuce in a medium bowl and toss in the shrimp mixture; serve immediately.

DID YOU KNOW ...

shrimp is the most popular shellfish in the United States?

Marinated Steak Nachos

10 to 12 servings

Imagine this: It's 11:53 P.M. and I've just gotten off the air after demonstrating my Tex-Mex book. Backstage I'm greeted with lots of hungry-looking faces, and I'm thinking that the one pound of leftover steak sitting in front of me isn't going to go very far unless I slice it mighty thin. So that's just what I did, then I tossed it on top of some nachos and added a bit of shredded cheese. Olé, it was the birth of steak nachos! And what a great way it is to stretch so little so far. Yes, you can do it, too. It's perfect for a hearty lunch or quick dinner. (Wait till you see how great it looks—check out color page G!)

NOTE
Feel free to use more or less cheese, or even a different kind, and sprinkle it with additional toppings like chopped green chilies, jalapeño peppers, olives, salsa, or sour cream.

½ cup lemon juice
2 tablespoons minced garlic
1 tablespoon dried oregano
1 tablespoon ground cumin
1 teaspoon salt
1 tablespoon black pepper
One 1½-pound beef flank steak
1 package (14 ounces) tortilla chips
2 cups (8 ounces) shredded Colby Jack cheese blend
2 large tomatoes, seeded and chopped
3 scallions, thinly sliced

In a 9" × 13" baking dish, combine the lemon juice, garlic, oregano, cumin, salt, and pepper. Add the flank steak, turning to coat completely. Cover and marinate in the refrigerator for 30 minutes. Preheat the broiler. Place the steak on a rimmed baking sheet; discard the marinade. Broil for 8 to 9 minutes per side for medium, or until desired doneness beyond that. Allow to cool for 10 minutes. Place on a cutting board and cut across the grain into thin slices, then cut into 1-inch pieces. Reduce the oven temperature to 350°F. Spread the tortilla chips over two large rimmed baking sheets, then top evenly with the sliced steak and sprinkle with the cheese. Bake for 5 to 6 minutes, or until the cheese has melted. Remove from the oven and slide onto a large platter, if desired; sprinkle with the tomatoes and scallions. Serve immediately.

DID YOU KNOW . . .

traditional marinating is done with a flavorful liquid? But with all the new dry spice rubs available now, we can get the same tastes in a whole new way!

Chili Lasagna

6 to 8 servings

One time when I was making my special lasagna . . . uh oh! I realized I didn't have enough meat sauce to finish. What I did have was a few cans of no-bean chili. So, guess what? Chili lasagna was created!

9 lasagna noodles
2 cans (15 ounces each) no-bean chili
1 container (15 ounces) ricotta cheese
3 cups (12 ounces) shredded sharp Cheddar cheese, divided
3 scallions, thinly sliced, divided
1 egg
½ teaspoon salt
½ teaspoon black pepper

NOTE
For a spicier dish, add some hot pepper sauce and/or chili powder to the canned chili before assembling the lasagna.

Preheat the oven to 350°F. Cook the lasagna noodles according to the package directions; drain. Coat a 9" × 13" baking dish with nonstick cooking spray; spread ¾ cup chili in the bottom of the dish. Place 3 noodles over the chili. In a medium bowl, combine the ricotta cheese, 2 cups Cheddar cheese, 2 sliced scallions, the egg, salt, and pepper; mix well. Place half of the mixture evenly over the noodles, then top with half of the remaining chili. Place 3 noodles over the chili, then top with the remaining cheese mixture. Place the remaining 3 noodles over the cheese mixture, then top with the remaining chili. Sprinkle the remaining 1 cup Cheddar cheese over the top. Cover tightly with alu-

98

minum foil and bake for 30 to 35 minutes, or until heated through and bubbly. Remove the foil and bake for 5 more minutes. Remove from the oven and sprinkle with the remaining sliced scallion. Allow to sit for 5 minutes before serving.

DID YOU KNOW . . .

this is an example of "fusion cuisine," also known as cross-cultural cooking? It's a dish or style of cooking that combines the foods or tastes of different areas. This one's a combination of Mexican and Italian cooking styles in one pan.

No-Bean Chili

4 to 6 servings

A few spices added to leftover ground beef (which we often have) and we've got a tasty beanless chili! It's ready to be served right from the bowl or ladled over our favorite pasta. By the way, there's nothing like a little spicy chili to keep the crew on their toes in the wee hours.

3 pounds ground beef
1 medium onion, chopped
3 garlic cloves, minced
3 tablespoons chili powder
2 teaspoons ground cumin
1 tablespoon hot pepper sauce
2 teaspoons salt
3 cups water
1 can (4.5 ounces) chopped green chilies, drained

NOTE
This is perfect in Chili Lasagna (page 98), or served over hot cooked rice and garnished with chopped onions, shredded cheese, and sour cream.

In a soup pot, cook the ground beef, onion, and garlic over medium-high heat for 8 to 10 minutes, or until the beef is browned and the onion is tender, stirring frequently. Stir in the chili powder, cumin, hot pepper sauce, and salt; cook for 1 minute. Add the water and chilies; bring to a boil, stirring occasionally. Cook for 40 to 45 minutes, or until thickened, stirring occasionally.

Sweet-and-Sour
Coleslaw

David Venable's
Baked Corn Casserole

Jane Rudolph Treacy
Rudy's Ribs

E

Chef's Salad Skewers

Pepperoni Pizza Dip in Bread Bowl

F

Marinated Steak Nachos

G

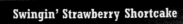

Swingin' Strawberry Shortcake

H

Asian Stir-Fry Omelet

4 to 6 servings

Since everybody's up so early at QVC, breakfast is huge. You know, they work around the clock there. So one time after I made a little extra stir-fry (actually a lot), I didn't know what to do with it, when it "dawned" on me to attempt a stir-fry omelet. It was, well, to quote the morning show team, "Awesome." See what your team thinks!

4 teaspoons sesame oil, divided
1 tablespoon hoisin sauce
1 tablespoon soy sauce
¼ teaspoon crushed red pepper
¼ pound fresh mushrooms, thinly sliced
8 asparagus spears, cut into 2-inch pieces
1 small onion, sliced
½ medium red bell pepper, chopped
8 eggs, beaten

> **DID YOU KNOW . . .**
> stir-frying means cooking small pieces of meat, poultry, fish, and/or vegetables over very high heat with very little oil? That makes it easier on our waistlines!

In a small bowl, combine 1 teaspoon sesame oil, the hoisin sauce, soy sauce, and crushed red pepper; mix well. Heat the remaining sesame oil in a large skillet over medium-high heat. Add the mushrooms, asparagus, onion, and bell pepper and stir-fry for 4 to 5 minutes. Add the hoisin sauce mixture and cook for 1 minute, until well coated. Reduce the heat to medium-low and pour the eggs over the vegetables. Cover and cook for 10 to 12 minutes, or until the top is set and the eggs are cooked through. Cut into wedges and serve immediately.

Chef's Salad Skewers

6 servings

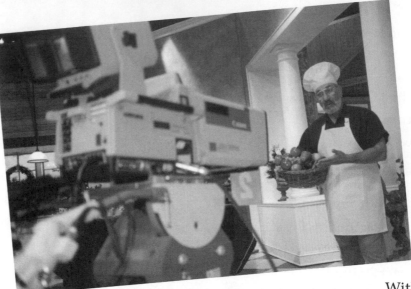

With people always running in so many directions in the QVC studio, it's not always easy to stop and eat lunch. Well, I certainly want to make sure the camera people are fed, since they're the ones who make me look so tall, dark, and handsome. So I created a special lunch just for them: chef's salad skewers. That way they can eat with one hand and work the camera with the other. Flip to the photo on color page F to see how portable these are.

4 slices (¼ pound) deli turkey
4 slices (¼ pound) deli ham
4 slices (2 ounces) Swiss or yellow Cheddar cheese
4 slices (¼ pound) deli roast beef

1 small head iceberg lettuce, cut into 12 chunks
1 large tomato, cut into 12 chunks

Six 10-inch skewers

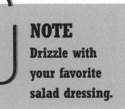

NOTE
Drizzle with your favorite salad dressing.

Place the slices of turkey on a work surface and top each with a slice of ham, a slice of cheese, and a slice of roast beef. Starting at the narrow end, roll up jelly-roll style and slice each roll into three equal pieces. Alternately thread each skewer with two pieces each of the meat and cheese roll, lettuce, and tomato. Serve immediately, or cover and chill until ready to serve.

DID YOU KNOW . . .

there's a really easy way to keep salad chilled on your serving table? Pour a small amount of water into a large bowl and freeze. When ready to serve, place the salad in a smaller bowl and place that bowl in the large bowl. Ta da! Cool, crisp salad for your serving table!

Creamy Chocolate Spread

about ½ cup

This spread started out as a joke, 'cause in my cookbook *"Help, Mr. Food®! Company's Coming!"* I have a bunch of different-flavored bagel spreads. Everybody always joked with me, telling me I'd left out the chocolate spread. And they were right—I had. I created this spread so that my chocoholic friends could enjoy a bit of smooth chocolate on their breakfast breads. See what you think . . .

1 package (3 ounces) cream cheese, softened
⅓ cup semisweet chocolate chips, melted
¼ cup firmly packed light brown sugar

In a small bowl, combine all the ingredients until well blended and smooth. Serve immediately, or cover and chill until ready to serve; allow to return to room temperature before serving.

Dave's always close by to help with those last-minute finishing touches.

NOTE
Use as a spread on toasted French bread slices, bagels, or even crackers with peanut butter.

Garlicky Breadsticks

1 dozen breadsticks

One time, when we were getting ready to have a last-minute production meeting, Dave Tinsch, who helps me prepare all the great-looking QVC food, brought out a big bowl of pasta and a basket of hot, crunchy breadsticks. The pasta was great, but the breadsticks were incredible. And when I heard how easy they were to make, I knew I had to share them with you. See for yourself how mouthwatering they look on color page L . . . then go for it!

DID YOU KNOW . . . garlic will stay fresh if stored in the freezer?

1 loaf (12 ounces) French bread
½ cup (1 stick) butter, melted
¼ cup chopped fresh parsley
6 garlic cloves, minced
½ teaspoon black pepper

Preheat the oven to 425°F. Cut the loaf of bread in half crosswise, then cut each piece lengthwise in half. Cut each of the four pieces into three long strips. In a small bowl, combine the remaining ingredients and brush on the strips of bread. Place on two baking sheets and bake for 5 to 6 minutes, or until golden. Serve warm.

NOTE These easy-to-make breadsticks can be seasoned with any of your favorite fresh or dried herbs.

The Green Room Special

4 sandwiches

There's never any shortage of food in the QVC Green Room—you know, the area where we hang out between shows. And since the folks at QVC are always so nice to provide my assistants and me with fresh fruit, bagels, and drinks, I decided to go a step further and share the idea for these special bagel sandwiches with other backstage guests. A little bit of homemade veggie cream cheese and some sliced turkey breast and we had a sandwich we dubbed "The Green Room Special." And, yes, you can make this one at home without painting your kitchen walls green.

1 package (8 ounces) cream cheese, softened
1 scallion, thinly sliced
½ small red bell pepper, finely chopped
1 teaspoon yellow mustard
¼ teaspoon salt
½ pound sliced deli turkey
4 bagels, split

In a small bowl, combine the cream cheese, scallion, bell pepper, mustard, and salt; mix well. Spread evenly over the cut sides of the bagels. Place the turkey in equal amounts over the bottom halves of the bagels, replace the tops, and serve.

DID YOU KNOW . . .

bagels, a commonplace breakfast food and sandwich bread around the country today, were once mainly eaten as a staple by Jewish immigrants?

Clam Chowder Casserole

4 to 6 servings

If you've never tried the clam chowder recipe from my *Real American* cookbook, you really have to. It was the starting point for this recipe, 'cause we combined leftover chowder with macaroni, topped it with shredded cheese, and baked it for a toss-together that's New England tasty.

1 package (8 ounces) elbow macaroni

2 cups (8 ounces) shredded sharp white Cheddar cheese

2 cans (10¾ ounces each) condensed New England clam chowder (see Note)

1 can (6½ ounces) minced clams, drained

2 scallions, thinly sliced

½ teaspoon black pepper

1 cup oyster crackers

1 tablespoon butter, melted

Preheat the oven to 375°F. Cook the macaroni according to the package directions; drain. Coat an 8-inch square baking dish with nonstick cooking spray. In a medium bowl, combine the macaroni, cheese, clam chowder, clams, scallions, and pepper; mix well. Pour into the baking dish, sprinkle evenly with the crackers, and drizzle with the butter. Bake for 25 to 30 minutes, or until bubbly and the topping is golden.

DID YOU KNOW . . .
Manhattan chowder has a tomato-based broth, while New England chowder is usually a creamy milk-based soup? What began as a regional preference is now simply a matter of taste preference.

NOTE
If you're watching your salt intake, try using a low-sodium clam chowder.

107

Program Guide

There sure is something to be said for that moment when a big brown package with the letters QVC printed all over it greets us on the front doorstep. Our first instinct is to pick it up and shake it. . . . Hmm, even though we already know what's in it, our excitement builds as we imagine what could possibly be inside. We tear into the box as if it's a surprise birthday present. We fold back the flaps of the box and dig through the packing material to find the buried treasure at the bottom. And, suddenly, there it is! The item we ordered has arrived safe and sound. But before we can do anything with it, the urge strikes again—you know, to dig through the sea of foam peanuts one more time, in search of whatever else might be hiding inside. Aha! There it is! No, not more merchandise, but another prize: the QVC Program Guide.

With that and our TV's remote control, we're in business. Yup, the Program Guide lets us know when to tune in to our favorite QVC shows, when to watch previews, and who's going to be visiting the studio each day. It makes us feel like we have some secret inside information, and with one glance it's obvious . . . boy, do we have program choices!

I know I'm not alone in feeling this way, 'cause in my travels I've heard of many groups of folks who throw QVC get-togethers. How do they work? Like this: A group of friends gathers at someone's house in front of the TV for a QVC pro-

gram party. It's like going shopping with friends, only better—
'cause we don't have to look for parking spots, drag our packages around with us, or even leave the comfort of home!

Of course, when we're home, we can't stop at the food
court, so it's nice to have munchies, or maybe dinner or dessert,
available for everybody . . . or we can even ask each person to
bring one dish. Instead of serving the same old thing, maybe
we can have foods that are related to the QVC shows that we're
going to watch. To make it all easier, I've put together some of
my favorite combos—foods that match our favorite QVC programs. Go ahead and sample mine, get a few others from iQVC
(QVC's Internet site), or come up with some of your own. After
all, we need energy if we're gonna be doing some serious shopping, don't we?!

Program Guide

Program Guide

"The QVC Morning Show"

Breakfast Sausage Ring

12 to 16 servings

In the mornings, when time allows, my wife and I like to watch the morning programs on TV. That's how we catch up on news and check the day's weather. Of course we end up channel surfing a bit before tuning in to *The QVC Morning Show*. What a way to start the day—with everything we want to see!

2 packages (1 pound each) hot pork sausage (see Note)

1½ cups coarsely crushed butter-flavored crackers

1 large apple, peeled, cored, and grated

1 small onion, grated

1 egg

2 tablespoons milk

Preheat the oven to 350°F. In a large bowl, combine all the ingredients; mix until well blended. Press firmly into a 10-inch Bundt or tube pan. Bake for 65 to 70 minutes, or until cooked through. Remove from the oven and pour off any liquid. Carefully place a plate over the top of the pan and invert onto a serving platter; serve warm.

DID YOU KNOW . . . you can substitute crushed crackers for bread crumbs in most recipes?

NOTE It's nice to fill the center of the ring with your favorite scrambled eggs—plain or with tomatoes, mushrooms, or Cheddar cheese. And make sure to use a finely ground pork sausage that comes in a tube, like Jimmy Dean® sausage.

6 servings

"Health & Fitness"

Italian Turkey Roll

These days it seems everyone's into health and fitness. Believe it or not, I exercise and do my stretching faithfully every morning. And, thanks to QVC, we've all learned about the latest types of exercise equipment available . . . and even learned a few new moves. We sure don't want to ruin all that hard work by not eating healthy. Don't worry, healthy food can be full of flavor! Take these turkey rolls, made with thinly sliced turkey, fresh tomatoes, basil, and seasonings—it's hard to believe that something so tasty can also be good for us! So move the laundry off your exercise bike, flip on QVC, and get cookin'!

4 plum tomatoes, finely chopped
¼ cup chopped fresh basil
6 garlic cloves, minced
½ teaspoon salt
¼ teaspoon black pepper
6 thinly sliced turkey breast cutlets (about 1½ pounds total)

Preheat the oven to 375°F. Coat an 8-inch square baking dish with nonstick cooking spray. In a small bowl, combine the tomatoes, basil, garlic, salt, and pepper; mix well. Place the turkey cutlets on a work surface; using half of the

114

tomato mixture, spread an equal amount of it over each cutlet, leaving a ¼-inch border. Starting from a smaller end, roll up jelly-roll style. Place the turkey rolls seam side down in the baking dish. Spread the remaining tomato mixture evenly over the top of the rolls. Bake for 35 to 40 minutes, or until no pink remains in the turkey.

DID YOU KNOW . . .

Benjamin Franklin wanted the turkey to be the national bird, instead of the bald eagle?

"Weekend Brunch"

4 to 6 servings

Scallion "Egg Roll"

One of my favorite weekend activities is a good old-fashioned brunch. I love having my family and close friends over to share good food and lots of laughs. It's fun to have a shopping brunch, too! How? Move the TV into the dining room or the food into the family room and get ready to enjoy this easy cheesy breakfast (shown on color page C) as you do your shopping at a nice leisurely pace.

        4 eggs
        1 cup milk
        ½ cup all-purpose flour
        ½ teaspoon salt
        ½ teaspoon black pepper
        5 scallions, thinly sliced
        1 cup (4 ounces) shredded Cheddar cheese

Preheat the oven to 350°F. Line a 9" × 13" rimmed baking sheet with aluminum foil, then coat the foil with nonstick cooking spray. In a large bowl, whisk together the eggs, milk, flour, salt, and pepper for 2 to 3 minutes, or until the mixture is smooth. Stir in the scallions, then pour the mixture onto the baking sheet. Bake for 12 to 15 minutes, or until set. Sprinkle evenly with the cheese, then bake for 2 to 3 minutes, or until the cheese has melted. Allow to cool for 5 minutes, then carefully lift the aluminum foil (eggs and all) and remove it from the baking sheet. Starting from a smaller end, roll up the eggs jelly-roll style, carefully releasing them from the aluminum foil as you roll. Slice into 1-inch pieces and serve.

NOTE Breakfast sausage and raisin toast are the perfect go-alongs to make this a complete brunch.

DID YOU KNOW . . .

it's better to add water than milk to scrambled eggs? Milk makes the yolks harder to break down, while water makes fluffier omelets.

"Now You're Cooking"

6 to 8 servings

Creamy Walnut Penne

This is right up my alley. In fact, I've shared the *Now You're Cooking* set many times with Bob Bowersox and lots of other hosts, and they sure do know how to whip up some tasty recipes. I created this recipe to celebrate all the fun we've all had over the years. You're invited to serve it any time you need a little something extra special. Your gang will surely say, "Now you're cooking!"

1 pound penne pasta
2 cups (8 ounces) shredded Italian cheese blend
2 cups (1 pint) heavy cream
1 cup chopped walnuts
1½ teaspoons salt
1 teaspoon black pepper
¼ cup chopped fresh parsley

DID YOU KNOW . . .

evaporated milk can be substituted for heavy cream in many of our favorite recipes? That way we get the same flavor, but less fat.

Cook the pasta according to the package directions; drain. In a large saucepan, combine the cheese, cream, walnuts, salt, and pepper; mix well. Add the pasta and cook over low heat until well combined and heated through. Remove from the heat. Stir in the parsley and serve immediately.

"Luck of the Irish"

Potato Apples

1 dozen "apples"

St. Patrick's Day is a fun time. There are parades and lots of tasty foods . . . why, it's an all-out party time! And every year you can count on indulging with lots of corned beef, cabbage, and, of course, potatoes. But instead of serving them boiled again, I came up with a new twist. Trust me, this idea will catch on quick with all the leprechauns in your kitchen.

    4 cups warm mashed potatoes (see Note)
    1 egg yolk
    1 teaspoon water
    ¼ teaspoon paprika
    12 whole cloves

Preheat the oven to 450°F. Coat a baking sheet with nonstick cooking spray. Shape the potatoes into twelve balls and place on the baking sheet. In a small bowl, beat the egg yolk, water, and paprika. Brush the mixture over the top of the potato balls. Insert the rounded end of a clove into the top of each potato ball, forming apple "stems." Bake for 10 to 12 minutes, or until golden. **Remove cloves before serving.**

DID YOU KNOW . . . we can add extra flavor and color to plain mashed potatoes by boiling them with carrots, beets, or spinach?

NOTE
Make sure the mashed potatoes are thick and firm so they'll form balls.

"The NFL™ Team Shop"

4 calzones

Reuben Calzones

There sure is something for everyone! When we're planning to get together with the gang to watch the big football game, we can get into the spirit by buying our favorite team's jerseys, hats, and other paraphernalia. Of course, when the excitement of the game is building, we're gonna want to feed our hungry fans. Why not give 'em these Reuben Calzones? They're hearty, they're tasty, and they're sure to get the gang shouting, "Rah, rah, QVC!"

> ½ pound sliced deli corned beef, chopped
> 1 can (14.4 ounces) sauerkraut, well drained
> ½ cup Thousand Island dressing
> 2 tubes (10 ounces each) refrigerated pizza dough
> 8 slices (6 ounces) Swiss cheese

Preheat the oven to 425°F. Coat two rimmed baking sheets with nonstick cooking spray. In a medium bowl, combine the corned beef, sauerkraut, and dressing; mix well. On a clean work surface, unroll the pizza dough, then cut each crosswise in half, making four rectangles. Place a slice of cheese at one end of each piece of dough, leaving a 1-inch border. Top the pieces of cheese with equal amounts of the corned beef mixture and place the remaining cheese slices over that. Fold the dough over the filling. With your fingers or a fork, pinch the edges together to seal. Place two calzones on each baking sheet. Coat the tops of the calzones with nonstick cooking spray and bake for 10 to 12 minutes, or until the crust is crisp and golden. Serve immediately.

DID YOU KNOW . . .
the NFL was formed way back in 1920?

"On Stage"

6 servings

Swingin'
Strawberry Shortcake

This swingin' strawberry shortcake is such a tempting treat that it should be *On Stage!* So turn up the music and start dancing to the beat with this fruity and creamy berry delight.

>   2 cups all-purpose flour
>   3 tablespoons granulated sugar, divided
>   1 tablespoon baking powder
>   ½ teaspoon salt
>   2 cups (1 pint) heavy cream, divided
>   1 tablespoon butter, melted
>   ¼ teaspoon ground cinnamon
>   3 tablespoons confectioners' sugar
>   1 teaspoon vanilla extract
>   1 quart fresh strawberries, washed, hulled, and sliced

Preheat the oven to 425°F. Coat a large baking sheet with nonstick cooking spray. In a large bowl, combine the flour, 2 tablespoons granulated sugar, the baking powder, and salt; mix well. Add 1 cup heavy cream; mix thoroughly. Place the dough on a lightly floured surface, knead lightly until smooth, and roll out to a ½-inch thickness. Using a 3-inch biscuit cutter, cut into six circles, rerolling the dough scraps if necessary. Place the dough circles on the baking sheet. In a small bowl, combine the butter, cinnamon, and the remaining 1 tablespoon granulated sugar; mix well and brush evenly over the dough circles. Bake for 15 to 20 minutes, or until golden. Remove to a wire rack to cool completely. In a medium bowl, with an electric beater on medium speed, beat the remaining 1 cup heavy cream, the confectioners' sugar, and vanilla until stiff peaks form. Cut each shortcake horizontally in half. Place the bottom halves on individual serving plates or a large serving platter and, using half of the sliced strawberries, then half of the whipped cream, top each shortcake bottom with berries and cream. Replace the top halves of the shortcake and top with the remaining strawberries and whipped cream. Serve, or cover loosely and chill until ready to serve.

DID YOU KNOW . . .

you can find the freshest strawberries by checking their tops? Look for ones with full red color, then sniff away, since the ripest strawberries are very fragrant, too. Stay away from berries with white tops and little or no scent.

"Christmas Shoppe"

about 4 dozen

Ginger Ornament Cookies

"Jingle Bells," "Silver Bells"—there are so many Christmas bells to remember that sometimes it starts my head ringing! Luckily, I can visit QVC's *Christmas Shoppe* for a few hints and gifts during the busy holidays. And I've got another little hint for you: These ornament cookies not only taste good, but fancied-up with a little ribbon, they make decorations that can really brighten up the tree. So make a few batches—one for giving, one for the tree, and one more for those cookie snitches who seem to show up while we're in the middle of our baking!

¾ cup (1½ sticks) butter, softened
1 cup sugar
2 eggs
2¾ cups all-purpose flour
2 teaspoons ground ginger
1 teaspoon ground cinnamon
¼ teaspoon ground nutmeg
¼ teaspoon ground cloves
¼ teaspoon salt

In a large bowl, with an electric beater on medium speed, combine the butter and sugar until fluffy. Beat in the eggs. In a medium bowl, combine the remaining ingredients; mix well. Gradually beat the flour mixture into the butter mixture until well combined. Form the dough into two balls and chill for about 1 hour. Preheat the oven to 350°F. Remove one dough ball at a time from the refrigerator. On a lightly floured surface, using a rolling pin, roll out the dough to a ¼-inch thickness. Using your favorite cookie cutters or a knife, cut into shapes and place carefully on ungreased baking sheets. Using a straw, make a hole near the top of each cookie (for threading the ribbon through later). Bake for 10 to 12 minutes, or until the edges are lightly golden. Allow to cool for 3 to 5 minutes, then remove to wire racks to cool completely.

NOTE
Thread a piece of your favorite colorful or sparkling ribbon through the hole in each cookie. Tie a knot in each so you can hang them on your Christmas tree. Remember, you can bake any type of sprinkles or miniature candies into the cookies or even decorate them with icings and glazes after baking.

DID YOU KNOW . . .

Christmas Day is the only day of the year that QVC does not air regular programming? That makes it a twenty-four-hour, 364-day-a-year operation!

"Company's Coming"

10 to 12 servings

Strawberry-Glazed Ham

Hearing somebody answer the phone, then yell, "Company's coming for dinner!" is enough to make even the most experienced host nervous, but with just a little help, entertaining can be a breeze. Why, with all the company that shows up at *my* front door, heaven knows I need all the help I can get! Here's one idea—a super-fancy dish that takes very little work. It's a glazed ham that looks as good as it tastes, and it's ideal for those times when you want the oven to do all the work.

One 5- to 6-pound fully cooked ham
2 cups strawberry jam
¼ cup yellow mustard

NOTE
For carving hints, check out the information on page 258.

Preheat the oven to 325°F. Coat a roasting pan with nonstick cooking spray; place the ham in the pan. With a knife, score the top and sides of the ham; bake for 1 hour. In a small bowl, combine the jam and mustard; mix well and pour over the ham. Bake for 30 to 35 minutes longer, or until heated through and glazed. Transfer to a serving platter and serve with the pan drippings on the side. Carve and serve.

"Your Country Home"

Catfish Stew

4 to 6 servings

As you know from my Southern cookbook, I love to cook Southern-style—and this catfish stew is proof that good ol' Southern country flavor is more popular than ever. You know, catfish isn't just a Southern fish anymore, 'cause now that it's farm-raised, we can get it just about everywhere.

1 tablespoon olive oil

1 large green bell pepper, cut into ½-inch chunks

1 medium onion, finely chopped

1 garlic clove, minced

2 cans (14½ ounces each) Italian-style stewed tomatoes

1 can (14½ ounces) ready-to-use chicken broth

2 bay leaves

1 teaspoon crushed red pepper

½ teaspoon dried thyme

1½ pounds catfish fillets, cut into 1-inch chunks

> **DID YOU KNOW . . .** farm-raised catfish is the freshest and cleanest type of catfish available?

In a soup pot, heat the olive oil over high heat. Add the bell pepper, onion, and garlic and cook for 5 to 6 minutes, or until tender, stirring frequently. Add the stewed tomatoes, broth, bay leaves, crushed red pepper, and thyme; mix well. Bring to a boil; cover and cook for 10 minutes. Add the fish, cover, and cook for 10 minutes, or until the fish flakes easily with a fork. **Remove the bay leaves and serve.**

"American Ingenuity"

8 servings

Italian Hoagies

When I was a kid, I walked five miles each way to and from school in the snow every winter morning. Only kidding! That's the story we tell our grandchildren. But it sure seemed that far . . . and, in my day, nobody ever got a ride to school. Thank goodness some things have changed for the better over the years, thanks to true American ingenuity. You know, with my busy schedule, it's not easy for me to keep up with all the gizmos and gadgets constantly appearing in the market-place, so it's good to know we can flip on *American Ingenuity* for updates on the latest and greatest. Oh—here's a true exam-ple of ingenuity done Mr. Food style. A hearty all-American hoagie rolled in a tortilla? Sure, it's an old-time taste with a contemporary twist. Pretty ingenious, wouldn't you say?

Eight 10-inch flour tortillas
½ pound sliced deli salami
½ pound sliced deli turkey
½ pound sliced deli ham
1 pound sliced provolone cheese (24 slices)
1 large tomato, diced
½ medium onion, diced
½ medium head iceberg lettuce, shredded
¾ cup Italian dressing

Place the tortillas on a work surface. Layer with the salami, turkey, ham, cheese, tomato, onion, and lettuce, leaving a ½-inch border around the edge of each tortilla. Pour the dressing over each and roll up tightly. Serve immediately.

NOTE
Serve with additional condiments like mayonnaise or mustard on the side.

DID YOU KNOW . . .

hoagie is another name for a submarine sandwich? Other popular names for this scrumptious combo: hero, Dagwood, and bomber.

"The Bed & Breakfast Inn"

4 to 6 servings

Monogram Pancakes

During our annual visits to Rhode Island, my wife and I always stay at a quaint bed and breakfast. One thing we've learned is how well they treat their guests! It's so comfortable, it's almost like visiting relatives . . . only better, 'cause there we get pampered! All I can say about those special breakfasts is, "Wow!" So of course I created these pancakes to make us feel bed-and-breakfast special at home any time at all.

> 1½ cups all-purpose flour
> ¾ cup vanilla yogurt
> ¾ cup milk
> ¼ cup (½ stick) butter, melted
> ¼ teaspoon baking powder
> ¼ teaspoon baking soda
> ¼ teaspoon salt

In a large bowl, whisk together all the ingredients until smooth. Pour into a large squeeze bottle (see Note). Heat a large nonstick skillet over medium-low heat. Squeeze the batter from the bottle to form your monogram in the skillet. Cook for 1 minute, or until set; turn over and cook for about 30 seconds, or until golden. Repeat with the remain-

130

ing batter, creating the same or different monograms. Serve with maple syrup.

NOTE
You can use a ketchup or mustard squeeze bottle from an outdoor cooking set, or another type of food squeeze bottle that has been emptied and cleaned well.

DID YOU KNOW . . .

that a product must contain at least 35 percent true maple syrup in order to be sold as maple syrup? If it's got less, with the rest sugarcane syrup or another type of sweetener, then it must be called pancake syrup. Check your labels!

"The Family Room"

6 servings

Big Burger

Evenings are the best time to gather the family for a night of TV and togetherness. I know that with everybody's busy schedules, it's hard to get together sometimes, so I invented this big burger that everyone can enjoy together. There are no individual burgers and messy toppings to worry about. All you have to do is roll out the blankets and grab a few pillows and a handful of napkins. Last but not least, tune in to *The Family Room* and sink your teeth into this juicy homemade super burger. (See how tempting it looks on color page M!)

> 1½ pounds lean ground beef
> 1 small onion, finely chopped
> 1 teaspoon salt
> 1 teaspoon black pepper
> ¼ pound Cheddar cheese, sliced
> 4 iceberg lettuce leaves
> One 8-inch round loaf Italian or white bread, cut
>   horizontally in half

Preheat the oven to 375°F. In a 9-inch pie plate, combine the ground beef, onion, salt, and pepper; mix well and form into a large hamburger patty. Bake for 30 minutes.

Remove from the oven and top with the cheese slices. Return to the oven and bake for 5 to 8 minutes, or until no pink remains in the ground beef and the cheese is melted. Place the lettuce leaves over the bottom half of the bread, then top with the burger. Replace the top of the bread, cut into wedges, and serve.

NOTE
Before cutting it into wedges, you can top this with your favorite condiments, like ketchup, mustard, mayonnaise, or pickles—or, if everybody likes something different, serve the toppers on the side.

DID YOU KNOW ...

we can pack more vitamins and nutrients into our diets by using darker-colored lettuces? Instead of making sandwiches and salads with iceberg, try romaine or other leafy green varieties.

"Halloween Special"

about 3 dozen

Candy Corn Cookies

Halloween sure is a favorite with my grandchildren. Why wouldn't it be? They get to dress up in clever costumes and prance around the neighborhood, filling up big bags with their favorite candy. I love this holiday, too—but there are lots of people who think that Halloween's only for kids. Not true! Try these candy corn cookies and see—adults and kids alike will love 'em.

> 1 package (18 ounces) refrigerated sugar cookie dough
> ¾ teaspoon yellow food color, divided
> 6 drops red food color

Divide the cookie dough in half; place half in a small bowl and add ¼ teaspoon yellow food color and the red food color; knead until the dough turns orange. Set aside 3 tablespoons of the uncolored dough; place the remaining uncolored dough in another small bowl. Add the remaining ½ teaspoon yellow food color; knead until the dough turns yellow. Roll each of the three pieces of dough into a 12-inch rope. Place the yellow dough rope on a piece of plastic wrap. Place the orange dough rope on the yellow one. Place the uncolored dough rope on the orange one. Using your hands, form the dough into a log that is triangular in shape, like candy corn. Cover with the plastic wrap and freeze for 1 hour. Preheat the oven to 350°F. Cut the frozen log into ¼-inch slices and place 2 inches apart on ungreased cookie sheets. Bake for 7 to 11 minutes, or until the edges are golden. Remove to a wire rack to cool completely.

DID YOU KNOW . . .

candy corn represents the corn our ancestors harvested every autumn?

"The Latest in Cooking"

4 servings

Easy Grilled Swordfish

Last year when I was at the National Housewares Show, I saw grill pans everywhere I turned. It seems they're "the latest in cooking" in kitchens everywhere. Wanna know the best part? We don't have to wait for nice weather to fire up the grill. We can grill in our kitchens with this easy recipe, an oh-so-tender grilled swordfish dish packed with flavor.

Juice of 2 lemons
½ cup vegetable oil
2 garlic cloves, minced
½ teaspoon salt
½ teaspoon black pepper
4 swordfish steaks (about 1½ pounds total), ½ inch thick

In a shallow dish, combine all the ingredients except the swordfish; mix well. Add the swordfish and turn to coat completely. Cover and marinate in the refrigerator for 1½ hours, turning occasionally. Coat a grill pan with nonstick cooking spray; preheat over medium-high heat. Remove the swordfish from the marinade; discard the marinade. Grill for 4 to 5 minutes per side, or until the fish flakes easily with a fork. Serve immediately.

DID YOU KNOW . . .

how to get the most juice from a lemon? Roll it gently but firmly on the counter with the palm of your hand. Place it in the microwave and heat on high power for 10 to 15 seconds. Cut in half and squeeze gently.

"Quick and Easy Cooking"

4 servings

Poached Asparagus and Salmon

Quick and Easy Cooking sounds familiar. Wait . . . isn't that what I do? It sure is, and here's a perfect example—an asparagus and salmon recipe that sounds fancy but, trust me, is really quick and easy. See for yourself!

4 salmon fillets (about 1½ pounds total)
1 teaspoon dried rosemary
½ teaspoon black pepper, divided
1 can (10½ ounces) condensed chicken broth
Juice of 1 lemon
½ pound fresh asparagus, trimmed and cut into 2-inch pieces

Season the salmon with the rosemary and ¼ teaspoon pepper and place in a large skillet. In a small bowl, combine the chicken broth, lemon juice, and the remaining ¼ teaspoon pepper; mix well and pour into the skillet. Place the asparagus around the salmon, cover, and bring to a boil over medium heat. Reduce the heat to low and simmer for 10 to 12 minutes, or until the fish flakes easily with a fork and the asparagus is tender. Serve immediately.

DID YOU KNOW . . .

asparagus season is from March to June? That's when we see lots of it in the supermarkets. And if it's not picked while still young, asparagus grows into tall, fern-like branches with bright red berries.

137

"Smart Cooking"

6 to 8 servings

Scallops and Mushrooms

These days smart cooking means fast and healthy cooking, too. Since so many of us are watching what we eat, sometimes we need a little expert advice. Luckily we have *Smart Cooking* to give us healthy meal preparation ideas and even offer us a few recipes. And here's one of my own, seafood with fresh vegetables. You can't get any smarter than that. Better send me to the head of the class!

¼ cup (½ stick) butter
½ pound fresh mushrooms, thinly sliced
2 garlic cloves, minced
1 can (10½ ounces) condensed chicken broth
1 medium head broccoli, cut into small florets
½ small red bell pepper, diced
1½ pounds sea scallops, quartered
3 tablespoons cornstarch
2 teaspoons soy sauce

Melt the butter in a large skillet over high heat. Add the mushrooms and garlic and sauté for 2 to 3 minutes, or until tender. Reserve ¼ cup chicken broth. Add the broccoli, bell pepper, and the remaining chicken broth to the skillet; mix well. Reduce the heat to medium and cook for 4 to 5 minutes, or until the broccoli is tender-crisp. Add the scallops and cook for 1 to 2 minutes, or until the scallops have turned white and are firm. In a small bowl, combine the cornstarch, soy sauce, and the reserved chicken broth until smooth; stir into the skillet and cook for 1 minute, or until thickened. Serve immediately.

DID YOU KNOW . . . the favorite pizza toppings in Japan are scallops and tuna?

Another stop on the QVC Studio Tour . . .

"Gems Galore"

about 4½ dozen

Dazzling Gem Cookies

As I waited to go on the air one time, I sat in the Green Room watching the end of *Gems Galore*. The glistening gem colors reminded me of these cookies that my grandchildren love. Though the gems in the cookies are nowhere near as valuable as the gems on QVC, they shine in their own way. So with very little work (and money), we can have our own display of rubies, emeralds, and topaz.

  ½ cup (1 stick) butter
  ½ cup vegetable shortening
  2½ cups all-purpose flour
  1 cup firmly packed light brown sugar
  1 egg
  1 teaspoon vanilla extract
  5 rolls (0.9 ounces each) Lifesavers®, separated by
      color and crushed

Preheat the oven to 375°F. Heavily coat two large cookie sheets with nonstick cooking spray. In a large bowl, combine all the ingredients except the Lifesavers®, stirring until a soft dough forms. On a lightly floured surface, roll out the dough to a ¼-inch thickness. Using a 2½-inch round cookie cutter, cut out cookies. Using a plastic soda bottle

140

cap, cut a 1-inch circle from the center of each cookie; carefully place the cookies on the cookie sheets. Fill each 1-inch center with about ½ teaspoon crushed candy. Bake for 6 to 8 minutes, or until the edges are golden. Allow to cool completely on the cookie sheets, then, using a large spatula, carefully remove the cookies and serve, or store in an airtight container.

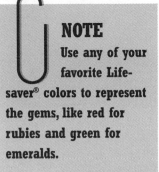

NOTE
Use any of your favorite Lifesaver® colors to represent the gems, like red for rubies and green for emeralds.

DID YOU KNOW . . .

Lifesavers® were created in 1912 and only came in one flavor then—peppermint?

"AM Style®"

4 to 6 servings

French Toast Loaf

Wow, QVC looks even bigger from up here!

Turn off the alarm clock, grab a cup of java, and start the day with a bit of *AM Style®*, the best guide to today's fashions. Not that I need them, since I'm a regular fashion plate. Ha, ha! Hey, I think I look pretty fashionable in my white apron and chef's hat. Anyway, I guess I should leave the fashion lessons up to you clotheshorses while I prepare a twist on old-fashioned French toast. You can see just how great it looks on color page B. Like this season's line, it's new, it's hot, and *"OOH IT'S SO GOOD!!®"*

DID YOU KNOW . . .

while Americans eat French toast for breakfast, the French eat it for dessert?

142

2 cups (1 pint) half-and-half

4 eggs

2 tablespoons sugar

1 teaspoon vanilla extract

1 teaspoon ground cinnamon

⅛ teaspoon ground nutmeg

4 cups bread cubes (see Note)

Preheat the oven to 350°F. Coat a 9" × 5" loaf pan with non-stick cooking spray. In a large bowl, combine all the ingredients except the bread cubes; mix well. Stir in the bread cubes and allow to sit for 10 minutes, or until all the liquid has been absorbed. Spoon into the loaf pan and bake for 55 to 60 minutes, or until golden. Remove from the pan, slice, and serve.

NOTE
You can use any type of leftover bread, and for a colorful loaf, you might even want to use a mixture of light and dark varieties. I like to top each slice with some confectioners' sugar and serve with maple syrup or fresh sliced fruit.

"Household Helpers"

8 to 10 servings

Processor Slaw

We're all looking for an extra pair of hands around the kitchen and, of course, *Household Helpers* that make life easier are always welcome. Here are the extra hands we've been looking for! No, those hands aren't live, they're mechanical—you know, a food processor. And trust me, a handy-dandy processor makes preparing this slaw easier than ever.

> 1 medium head green cabbage, quartered
> 2 carrots, peeled
> ½ small onion
> ¾ cup mayonnaise
> ½ cup vegetable oil
> ⅓ cup cider vinegar
> 1 tablespoon yellow mustard
> 3 tablespoons sugar
> 1 teaspoon salt
> ¼ teaspoon black pepper

Using a food processor fitted with its shredding disk, shred the cabbage, carrots, and onion, processing each separately. Place in a large bowl; mix well. In a small bowl, whisk the remaining ingredients until smooth and well combined.

Add to the cabbage mixture; mix well. Cover and chill for at least 2 hours before serving.

DID YOU KNOW . . .
cabbage picked after a hard winter frost is the sweetest?

"Picture Perfect®"

1 dozen cups

Homemade
Peanut Butter Cups

The words *Picture Perfect* and peanut butter cup may not seem like they belong together, but, trust me, in this case they sure do! I love the flavor of chocolate and peanut butter together so much that I created these jumbo-sized yummies that taste just as good as they look . . . *Picture Perfect!* (Wait till you see them on color page 0!)

1 package (11½ ounces) milk chocolate chips, divided
3 tablespoons vegetable shortening, divided
1½ cups confectioners' sugar
1 cup creamy peanut butter
¼ cup (½ stick) butter, softened

Line a 12-cup muffin tin with paper baking cups. In a small saucepan, melt 1¼ cups chocolate chips and 2 tablespoons shortening over low heat, stirring just until the mixture is smooth. Allow to cool slightly; the mixture should still be pourable. With the back of a spoon, coat the bottom half of each cup with about 2 teaspoons of the mixture. Chill for about 30 minutes, until firm. In a large bowl, combine the confectioners' sugar, peanut butter, and butter; mix well (the mixture will be stiff). Spoon evenly into the chocolate cups and press down firmly. In a small saucepan, melt the remaining ¾ cup chocolate chips and 1 tablespoon shortening over low heat, stirring just until the mixture is smooth. Spoon equally into the cups, spreading to cover the peanut butter mixture completely. Cover and chill for at least 2 hours, or until firm.

DID YOU KNOW ...

most commercially produced candy bars have an average shelf life of one year?

"Autumn Weekend"

Apple Crisp Tart

As the seasons change, we think of the perfect *Autumn Weekend* of picking apples, drinking warm apple cider, and snuggling by a cozy fire. Well, thoughts of all the leaves that are waiting to be raked won't leave me alone, either. Luckily, QVC's *Autumn Weekend* is brimming with distractions and even more great ways to avoid those leaves. So let's make a tasty fall dessert packed with apples. After that, I suppose it'll be time to finally get to those leaves . . . before the snow falls.

2¼ cups plus 2 tablespoons all-purpose flour, divided
½ cup (1 stick) plus 2 tablespoons butter, softened, divided
½ cup heavy cream
1 egg yolk
1 teaspoon salt
¾ cup firmly packed light brown sugar, divided
2 teaspoons ground cinnamon, divided
5 Red Delicious apples, peeled, cored, and thinly sliced

Preheat the oven to 350°F. Coat a 10" × 15" rimmed baking pan with nonstick cooking spray. In a medium bowl, combine 2 cups flour, ½ cup butter, the heavy cream, egg yolk, and salt; mix until a soft dough forms. Press evenly over the bottom and up the sides of the pan to form a crust. In a large bowl, combine ½ cup brown sugar, 2 tablespoons flour, and 1 teaspoon cinnamon; mix well. Add the apples and toss until well coated. Spread evenly over the dough. In a small bowl, using a fork, combine the remaining ¼ cup flour, ¼ cup brown sugar, 2 tablespoons butter, and 1 teaspoon cinnamon until crumbly. Sprinkle over the apples and bake for 40 to 45 minutes, or until the apples are tender and the crust is golden. Allow to cool slightly and serve warm.

DID YOU KNOW . . .

not all apples are created equal? Different apple varieties are best used for different things. For instance, Cortland, Crispin, Golden Delicious, and Granny Smith are great for baking, while Macoun and McIntosh are super for applesauce and candy and caramel apples! Of course, you can always use the ones you like best.

"Easter Basket Special"

2 dozen

Easter Egg Cookies

Easter is one of my favorite times to visit QVC 'cause everyone is hopping with excitement in anticipation of the Easter Bunny's visit. Here's something of mine that's pretty "egg"ceptional, too—Easter egg cookies. These colorful cookies are just as pretty as an Easter basket and a whole lot easier to put together.

>   2¼ cups all-purpose flour
>   1 cup sugar
>   ¾ cup (1½ sticks) butter, softened
>   1 egg
>   1 teaspoon vanilla extract
>   ⅛ teaspoon salt
>   4 food colors of your choice
>   Assorted sprinkles

Preheat the oven to 350°F. Coat two large rimmed cookie sheets with nonstick cooking spray. In a large bowl, combine the flour, sugar, butter, egg, vanilla, and salt; mix well. Using your hands, knead until a smooth dough forms. Divide the dough into four equal pieces. Add 2 to 3 drops of

a different food color to each piece of dough; work the color into the dough until the color is uniform through-out the dough. Divide each piece of colored dough into six pieces. Using your hands, shape each piece to look like an egg. Place the shaped dough about 1 inch apart on the cookie sheets and, using the palm of your hand, press flat. Decorate with the sprinkles and bake for 10 to 12 minutes, or until golden around the edges. Allow to cool slightly, then remove to a wire rack to cool completely.

DID YOU KNOW . . .

oven temperatures can vary a great deal? To be sure yours is cooking at the temperature it's set to, have it calibrated about once a year, or anytime your food seems to be cooking faster or slower than usual.

"Great Gifts"

about 3 dozen pieces

Raspberry Pistachio Fudge

Wait till you see all the great stuff you can pick up at the Studio Store!

Everyone needs a little help picking out *Great Gifts*, especially at holiday time. So one year I created this holiday fudge to give to each of my friends who has a sweet tooth. It's a raspberry and pistachio holiday fudge. Not only does its green and red color make it holiday perfect, so does its taste.

DID YOU KNOW . . .

chocolate is the most popular flavor of fudge, with vanilla and maple close behind?

1 container (16 ounces) strawberry-flavored frosting
2 packages (6 ounces each) white baking bars
¼ cup seedless raspberry jam
¾ cup pistachio nuts, coarsely chopped

Line an 8-inch square baking dish with aluminum foil. In a medium saucepan, combine all the ingredients except the nuts. Heat over medium heat and stir until the baking bars have melted and the mixture is smooth. Remove from the heat and stir in the nuts. Pour into the baking dish and chill for 1 to 2 hours, or until firm. Cut into squares and serve.

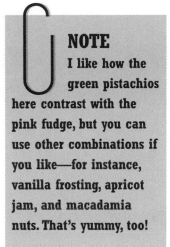

NOTE
I like how the green pistachios here contrast with the pink fudge, but you can use other combinations if you like—for instance, vanilla frosting, apricot jam, and macadamia nuts. That's yummy, too!

"Home Cooking"

6 to 8 servings

Chicken Potpie

Everyone loves *Home Cooking*, right? Of course we do. The smell alone is enough to make our mouths water in anticipation. You've gotta try my own home cookin' recipe for chicken potpie. It's filled with home-style flavor and it gets a big thumbs-up for looks, too!

¼ cup (½ stick) butter
¼ cup all-purpose flour
1 can (10½ ounces) condensed chicken broth
1 cup milk
1 teaspoon salt
½ teaspoon black pepper
1 package (15 ounces) folded refrigerated pie crust
   (2 crusts)
3 cups cubed cooked chicken
1 package (16 ounces) frozen peas and carrots, thawed
1 egg, beaten

Preheat the oven to 425°F. Coat a 9-inch deep-dish pie plate with nonstick cooking spray. In a medium saucepan, melt the butter over medium-high heat. Stir in the flour and cook for 1 to 2 minutes, or until light brown. Add the broth, milk, salt, and pepper; mix well. Bring to a boil, then remove from the heat. Unfold one pie crust and place in the pie plate, pressing the crust firmly against the plate. Sprinkle the chicken into the crust, then sprinkle in the peas and carrots. Pour the broth mixture over the peas and carrots, then place the remaining pie crust over the mixture. Trim and pinch the edges together to seal, and flute, if desired. Brush the beaten egg over the top. Using a sharp knife, cut four 1-inch slits in the top. Bake for 40 to 45 minutes, or until the crust is golden. Allow to sit for 10 minutes before serving.

DID YOU KNOW . . .

potpies have been around since 1792, yet the first frozen ones weren't produced until 1951, by the C. A. Swanson Company?

"Time Savers"

8 servings

Stuffed Breast of Turkey

Most of us hear *Time Savers* and boy, do we perk up! Between work, kids, the house, and errands, who has time to prepare big old-fashioned dinners anymore? Okay, I've got a recipe here that gives us the comforting tastes of home without hours of preparation. Actually, we'll be done putting it together in minutes, so let's turn on QVC and see if we can pick up more *Time Savers*.

> 1 package (8 ounces) corn bread stuffing, divided
> 1 can (8 ounces) water chestnuts, drained and chopped
> ⅔ cup hot water
> 2 tablespoons butter
> 8 turkey breast cutlets (about 2 pounds total), slightly pounded
> 2 jars (12 ounces each) turkey gravy
> 2 tablespoons chopped fresh parsley

Preheat the oven to 350°F. Coat a 9" × 13" baking dish with nonstick cooking spray. In a large bowl, combine 2 cups stuffing, the water chestnuts, hot water, and butter; mix well. Place the turkey cutlets on a work surface and place an equal amount of the stuffing mixture in the center of each piece of turkey; roll each turkey breast tightly, tucking in the sides as you roll. Place the rolls seam side down in the

156

baking dish. Pour the gravy over the bundles and sprinkle the remaining corn bread stuffing over the top. Cover tightly with aluminum foil and bake for 45 minutes. Remove the foil and bake for 10 to 15 more minutes, or until heated through and no pink remains in the turkey. Sprinkle with the parsley and serve.

DID YOU KNOW . . .

QVC is available in more than sixty-four million cable and satellite homes, helping millions of people save loads of shopping time?

Talk about Time Savers . . . let me introduce you to Katie— a working mom who's a real whiz in the kitchen. She appears on my show from time to time, sharing all kinds of tasty, time-saving tips.

"For the Guys"

4 to 6 servings

Beer-Soaked Buffalo Wings

QVC's got so many great shows! *Gems Galore* appeals mostly to the gals and *For the Guys* is, well, just like it says—for the guys. It's where we learn about tools, cars, and all that other "guy stuff." What better snack to serve than some hearty beer-soaked Buffalo wings?! By adding beer and spices to regular chicken wings, we get a new kind of wing. They're so awesome we'd better make some for the guys *and* the gals.

2 cans (12 ounces each) beer
1 package (5 pounds) frozen chicken wings, thawed
2 teaspoons ground red pepper
1 teaspoon salt
¾ cup cayenne pepper sauce (see Note)
¼ cup (½ stick) butter, melted

Measure out ⅓ cup beer and set aside. Pour the remaining beer into a large shallow dish; add the chicken wings, cover, and refrigerate for at least 4 hours; drain. Preheat the oven to 425°F. Line two large rimmed baking sheets with aluminum foil and coat the foil with nonstick cooking spray.

158

Season the wings with the ground red pepper and salt and place on the baking sheets. Bake for 30 minutes. Turn the wings over and cook for 25 to 30 more minutes, or until crispy and no pink remains. In a large bowl, combine the cayenne pepper sauce, butter, and the reserved beer; mix well. Add the chicken wings and toss until evenly coated. Serve immediately.

NOTE
Make sure to use *cayenne* pepper sauce instead of plain hot pepper sauce because that would make these *really* spicy.

DID YOU KNOW . . .

beer is a tasty marinade for meat, chicken, and seafood, as well as an excellent tenderizer?

I think I'll stick to cooking . . .

159

"All Plugged In"

5 to 6 servings

Pork Stew

Ever wander around the cooking section of a department store? There are so many appliances out there and, these days, most of them are *All Plugged In*. One of my favorites is also one of the most overlooked, the slow cooker, otherwise known as a Crock-Pot. It just makes our lives so much easier when we can put our meal together in the morning and have it ready when we get home.

3 medium potatoes, peeled and cut into 1-inch chunks
3 carrots, peeled and cut into 1-inch chunks
3 medium apples, peeled, cored, and quartered
1 medium onion, cut into wedges
1 teaspoon salt
1 teaspoon black pepper
2 pounds boneless pork roast or butt, cut into 1½-inch chunks
1 cup beef broth
2 tablespoons water
2 tablespoons cornstarch
2 teaspoons browning and seasoning sauce

In a 3½-quart (or larger) slow cooker, combine the potatoes, carrots, apples, onion, salt, and pepper. Place the pork on top and pour the broth over it. Cover and cook on the high setting for 5 to 6 hours. In a small bowl, combine the water, cornstarch, and browning and seasoning sauce; mix well. Stir into the stew until thickened and serve.

DID YOU KNOW . . .

adding a splash or two of red wine to our stews gives them an extra flavor boost?

"Patio & Garden"

6 to 8 servings

Garden Pie

My neighbor is a huge fan of gardening, and he sure does a good job in his yard. Every time I turn my head, he has a new gadget, and I think he picks 'em up from the *Patio & Garden* shop. I have no problem leaving the real gardening to him, 'cause I'd rather make garden pie. You don't need a green thumb for this one.

1 package (12 ounces) semisweet chocolate chips, melted
1 container (8 ounces) frozen whipped topping, thawed
1½ cups coarsely crushed chocolate sandwich cookies
One 9-inch chocolate graham cracker pie crust
Fresh mint sprigs for garnish
Gummy worms for garnish

DID YOU KNOW . . . pies actually came to America with the Pilgrims and were served at the first Thanksgiving dinner?

Place the melted chocolate in a large bowl and allow to cool slightly. Add the whipped topping; mix well. Stir 1¼ cups crushed cookies into the chocolate mixture, then spoon into the pie crust. Sprinkle the remaining ¼ cup crushed cookies evenly over the top. Cover and chill for at least 2 hours. Garnish with rows of mint sprigs to resemble the beginning of a garden and add a few gummy worms for color.

"Sweet Treats"

Rocky Road Bars

about 3 dozen

When we think of something to give our sweethearts, sweets top the list. Our main sweethearts deserve nothing but the best, so I created this very special recipe for them. Don't forget to make a double batch, 'cause even though we may be giving these *Sweet Treats* to our sweethearts, this is one recipe they may not want to share.

  2¼ cups miniature marshmallows
  1 package (12 ounces) semisweet chocolate chips
  ½ cup creamy peanut butter
  2 tablespoons butter
  2 tablespoons finely chopped peanuts

Coat an 8-inch square baking dish with nonstick cooking spray. Place the marshmallows evenly over the bottom of the baking dish; set aside. In a medium saucepan, melt the chocolate chips with the peanut butter and butter over low heat, stirring constantly until smooth. Pour over the marshmallows, spreading to completely cover them. Sprinkle the peanuts over the top, cover, and chill for 2 hours. Cut into bars and serve, or keep refrigerated until ready to serve.

DID YOU KNOW . . .
we can make camp-style s'mores all year-round? We can simply heat a few marshmallows in the microwave for 20 seconds and sandwich them between graham crackers with a piece of a chocolate bar. Mmm, mmm!

"Out N' About"

6 to 8 servings

Mashed Potato Casserole

Say good-bye to messy spills and cold cooked foods because, thanks to *Out N' About,* we have lots of help storing and transporting everything. Try making this casserole to take along to potluck suppers or get-togethers with the gang. You'll love having it steamin'-ready when you get where you're going.

> 5 pounds potatoes, peeled and cut into chunks
> 1 package (8 ounces) cream cheese, softened
> ½ small onion, minced
> 2 eggs
> 2 tablespoons all-purpose flour
> 2 tablespoons chopped fresh parsley
> 1½ teaspoons salt
> 1 teaspoon black pepper
> 1 can (2.8 ounces) French-fried onions, coarsely chopped

Preheat the oven to 325°F. Place the potatoes in a soup pot and add just enough water to cover them. Bring to a boil over high heat, then reduce the heat to medium and cook for 12 to 15 minutes, or until fork-tender; drain. Coat a 2-quart casserole dish with nonstick cooking spray. In a large bowl, with an electric beater on medium speed, beat the potatoes and cream cheese until smooth. Add the onion, eggs, flour, parsley, salt, and pepper; continue beating until thoroughly blended, then spoon into the casserole dish. Sprinkle with the French-fried onions and bake for 35 to 40 minutes, or until heated through and the edges are golden.

DID YOU KNOW ...

for extra-creamy regular mashed potatoes, we can add some cream cheese and beat them for 4 to 5 minutes with an electric beater?

"Fun & Leisure"

about 1½ pounds

Saltwater Taffy

With all the traveling I do, you can be sure that *Fun & Leisure* are at the top of my list when I get time off. I recently had an old-fashioned taffy pull with my grandchildren and oh, what a ball we had! It's a great party idea and the best part is that everybody can pitch in. Some can mix, others can pull, the rest can wrap, and then, of course, everybody gets to chew!

    2 cups sugar
    1 cup light corn syrup
    1 cup water
    1½ teaspoons salt
    2 tablespoons butter
    1 teaspoon vanilla extract
    6 drops yellow food color

Coat a large rimmed baking sheet with nonstick cooking spray. In a medium saucepan, combine the sugar, corn syrup, water, and salt over medium heat, stirring until the sugar dissolves. Stop stirring and continue cooking until the mixture reaches the hard crack stage (see Note on page 239). Remove from the heat and stir in the butter, vanilla, and food color; mix well, then pour in a thin layer onto the baking sheet. Allow to cool for 10 minutes, or until cool enough to handle. With buttered hands, roll the taffy into a ball and pull for 15 to 20 minutes, or until it becomes hard to pull and pale yellow in color. Cut into 4 pieces and stretch into long strips that are ½ inch thick, then cut into bite-sized pieces. Wrap each piece in a small piece of waxed paper and twist the ends to seal.

DID YOU KNOW ...

how saltwater taffy got its name? The most popular story is that an ocean wave hit an Atlantic City taffy stand in the 1800s, completely drenching its stock with ... you guessed it—saltwater!

"The QVC Sampler"

about 3 dozen

Broccoli Cheese Bites

Sometimes we get tired of serving the same things week after week. We need fresh ideas and, as the saying goes, "Variety is the spice of life." So why not serve a sampler plate—you know, with a little of this and a little of that, just like *The QVC Sampler*? And here's a little something to get you started.

2 packages (10 ounces) frozen chopped broccoli, thawed and well drained

2 cups herb stuffing, crushed

1 cup grated Parmesan cheese

5 eggs

½ cup milk

½ cup (1 stick) butter

1 small onion, finely chopped

DID YOU KNOW . . . as part of a healthy diet, broccoli is one of the best sources of calcium?

Preheat the oven to 375°F. In a large bowl, combine the broccoli, crushed stuffing, Parmesan cheese, eggs, and milk; mix well and set aside. In a medium skillet, melt the butter over medium heat. Add the onion and sauté until tender. Add to the broccoli mixture; mix well. Shape into 1-inch balls and place on ungreased baking sheets. Bake for 15 to 20 minutes, or until golden and firm. Serve immediately.

"Big Bold Gold®"

Gold Bar

10 to 12 servings

When some people think of gold, they think of shiny necklaces, big earrings, and chunky bracelets. I guess I must be the exception, since I think of my recipe for an edible *Big Bold Gold* bar. Though it may not glisten the same way, it's the goldest, richest bar around.

> **DID YOU KNOW . . .**
> QVC is one of the world's largest gold retailers?

1 package (0.25 ounces) unflavored gelatin

1¾ cups warm milk

1 package (4-serving size) vanilla pudding and pie filling mix (*not* instant pudding)

1 package (11 ounces) butterscotch-flavored chips

Coat a 9" × 5" glass loaf dish with nonstick cooking spray. In a large saucepan, combine the gelatin and milk until the gelatin has dissolved. Slowly stir in the pudding mix; mix well. Bring to a boil over medium heat and boil for 3 minutes, stirring constantly. Add the butterscotch chips and cook for 1 to 2 minutes, or until the chips have melted and the mixture is smooth, stirring constantly. Pour into the loaf dish, cover, and chill for 3 to 4 hours, or until firm. Using a knife, loosen the "bar" from the sides of the dish and invert onto a serving platter. Cut and serve.

> **NOTE**
> Use a bottle of squeezable chocolate syrup to write "14 karat" or a personalized message on top of the "bar."

169

"Practical Presents"

Seasoning Blends

The best gifts are ones that can be used over and over again. So how 'bout making a big batch of these special seasonings that store well and are great to have on hand for adding flavor to everything from chicken to popcorn? You'll love them for yourself, and you can even put them in decorative containers to make super *Practical Presents* for the holidays that are really quite affordable, too.

Italian Seasoning

about ½ cup

3 tablespoons dried marjoram (optional)
2 tablespoons dried oregano
2 tablespoons dried thyme
1 tablespoon dried basil
1 tablespoon rubbed sage
1½ teaspoons dried rosemary
1 teaspoon garlic powder
1 teaspoon salt

NOTE
Use to season your favorite foods by lightly brushing meats, poultry, or seafood with some vegetable oil, then seasoning with the blend of your choice. Bake, broil, sauté, or grill as desired. It's best to pour out just as much of a seasoning blend as you plan to use, since you must discard any leftover blend that has come in contact with raw meat, poultry, or other foods.

Poultry Seasoning

about ¹/₂ cup

¼ cup paprika
1 tablespoon rubbed sage
2 teaspoons garlic powder
2 teaspoons onion powder
¼ teaspoon ground nutmeg
1 tablespoon salt
1 tablespoon black pepper

Cajun Spice

about ²/₃ cup

¼ cup paprika
2 tablespoons dried thyme
1 tablespoon onion powder
1 tablespoon garlic powder
1 tablespoon sugar
2 teaspoons ground red pepper
1 tablespoon salt
1 tablespoon black pepper

DID YOU KNOW . . .

QVC has taken orders for almost $30 million worth of merchandise in a single day?!

In a small bowl, combine all the ingredients for a particular seasoning blend; mix well. Store in an airtight container or resealable storage bag until ready to use.

"The Finishing Touch"

Garnishing Tips

Ta da! It's the finishing touches that make our homes and recipes complete. And what better way to finish off this chapter than with some garnishing tips to help dress up all the recipes we've made? And the bonus? These garnishes are edible, which makes 'em even better.

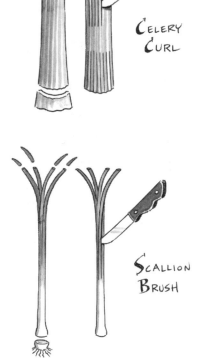

CELERY CURL

SCALLION BRUSH

1. *Celery Curls* Cut the ends of each piece of celery into very thin 1-inch strips, leaving the center portion of each piece uncut. Place in ice water and chill for at least 2 hours, or until the ends curl. Store in the ice water until ready to use. Drain well before using.
2. *Scallion Brushes* Trim the root end of each scallion. Trim the green tops so that they are all the same length, then cut the tops into narrow strips, starting from ½ inch above the joint. Place the root end of the scallions in ice water and chill for at least 2 hours, or until the green tips curl. Store in the ice water until ready to use. Drain well before using.
3. *Radish Chrysanthemums* Trim the root and stem ends from a few radishes. Place one radish at a time between two skewers on a flat surface. Cut the radish crosswise into ⅛-inch slices, using the skewers as guides to stop the knife from slicing completely through the radish.

Turn the radish 90 degrees (so that the cuts are parallel with the skewers); cut the radish into ⅛-inch slices at right angles to the first cuts. Place in ice water and chill for at least 2 hours, or until the "flowers" open. Store in the ice water until ready to use. Drain well before using.

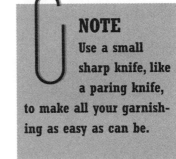

NOTE
Use a small sharp knife, like a paring knife, to make all your garnishing as easy as can be.

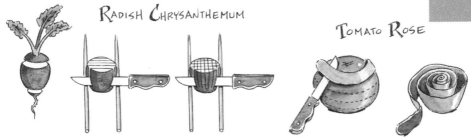

RADISH CHRYSANTHEMUM

TOMATO ROSE

4. *Tomato Roses* With a sharp paring knife, starting at the top of each firm, red tomato, remove the peel in one continuous 1-inch-wide spiral strip. Loosely roll each peel around itself to form a rose. Use fresh parsley to accent the roses.

173

Mailbag

I get so much mail from my many viewers . . . and I love it! Sometimes I get so wrapped up in reading all the questions, comments, and suggestions I get on a regular basis that I forget all about my personal mail! After all, why would I want to open bills, when I can read letters from my friends around the country? People write to me about all sorts of things, from requesting lost family recipes and telling me how I've saved their marriage by providing them with kitchen solutions to sending me recipes they've created and want to share. So I thought I would take this opportunity to include some letters from my mailbag and maybe inspire a few more letters, since I learn so much from all of you, too!

Mailbag

Mailbag

*I'm sure glad **I** don't have to deliver all these packages!*

Coffee Slushiccino

4 to 6 servings

Everybody's crazed for coffee these days, and I'm getting loads of requests for the homemade versions of those icy concoctions, steamy mochaccinos, and every other type of "cinos" that are served at the popular coffee houses. So I want to share my favorite one—I call it a "slushiccino." The best part besides the taste? We can make it at home for a fraction of what it costs at a coffee bar!

¾ cup heavy cream
¼ cup water
¼ cup instant coffee granules
¼ cup sugar
3 cups ice

NOTE To make a mocha slush, add 2 to 3 tablespoons chocolate syrup along with the coffee.

In a blender, combine the heavy cream, water, coffee granules, and sugar; blend until well mixed. Add the ice and blend until well combined and slushy. Serve immediately.

DID YOU KNOW . . .

the best way to get the freshest cup of coffee every time is to start by brewing cold water instead of warm? And never let the coffee sit for more than 30 minutes.

Dutch Apple Pie

6 to 8 servings

I'm often asked, "What's the difference between traditional apple pie and Dutch apple pie?" That's pretty easy to answer: Traditional apple pie is just that, traditional. You know, with a flaky top crust. Dutch apple pie is different because it's got a sugary, buttery crumb topping that gets crispy when baked. Now why not try this Dutch version so you can decide for yourself which is your personal favorite?

1 cup all-purpose flour, divided

¾ cup sugar

1 teaspoon ground cinnamon

4 large Granny Smith apples, peeled, cored, and cut into ½-inch slices

One 9-inch frozen ready-to-bake deep-dish pie shell, thawed

½ cup firmly packed light brown sugar

¼ cup (½ stick) butter, softened

DID YOU KNOW . . . the easiest way to peel apples is to carefully pour scalding water over them, drain, and peel 'em once they're cool?

Preheat the oven to 400°F. In a large bowl, combine ⅓ cup flour, the sugar, and cinnamon; mix well. Add the apples and toss to coat; spoon into the crust. In a small bowl, combine the remaining ⅔ cup flour, the brown sugar, and butter until crumbly. Sprinkle over the apples. Place the pie on a baking sheet and bake for 45 to 50 minutes, or until bubbly and the apples are tender. Remove to a wire rack to cool. Serve warm, or allow to cool completely before serving.

NOTE My favorite way to serve this pie is warm with a scoop of vanilla ice cream.

Doggie Bones

about 1 dozen biscuits

Over the years, it seems I've helped out every member of the family by providing recipes to home cooks via mail—and, recently, the Internet. Now, with this recipe, I get to provide a treat for the extra member of the family! These homemade doggie bones should make Buddy and Lucky doggone happy . . . and Murphy the QDog, too! They can even be made in different shapes and sizes, depending on the size of your pooch. Just wait till you see how much they like 'em! Why, they'll bark out their own version of *"OOH IT'S SO GOOD!!®"*

1 cup all-purpose flour
1 cup whole-wheat flour
½ cup wheat germ
½ cup powdered milk
3 tablespoons vegetable shortening
1 teaspoon brown sugar
½ teaspoon salt
1 egg
⅓ cup water

Preheat the oven to 350°F. Coat a cookie sheet with non-stick cooking spray. In a large bowl, combine both flours, the wheat germ, powdered milk, shortening, brown sugar, and salt; mix until crumbly. Add the egg and water; mix well. On a lightly floured surface, knead the dough until

180

smooth. Using a rolling pin, roll out to a ½-inch thickness. Using a dog bone–shaped cookie cutter or a knife, cut out biscuits. Place the biscuits about 1 inch apart on the cookie sheet and bake for 25 to 30 minutes, or until lightly browned. Remove to a wire rack to cool completely.

DID YOU KNOW . . .

QVC has a new host? His name is Murphy the QDog, and you'll be seeing lots more of him on air.

NOTE
I know dogs love these treats because we tested them . . . and our testers couldn't get enough of them! Oh, don't worry if the kids (or even adults) get into them—they're perfectly edible, but not very tasty to us. Just beware of any of your dog's possible existing allergies to wheat, eggs, or dairy products.

Happy-go-lucky Murphy loves to play ball, take long naps by the fire, and greet Studio Tour visitors. And, just like us, Murphy likes a crunchy treat now and then.

Chocolate-Almond Caramel Apples

4 apples

DID YOU KNOW . . .

candy apples have always been so popular at fairs and carnivals that now there are easy-to-make candy apple kits available in the produce section of most supermarkets?

One viewer wrote: "I'm a true QVC viewer—I watch it all the time. So, I'll admit, I've bought my fair share of those big caramel apples. They make great gifts and do they ever taste good! Unfortunately, they're not always available. Do you have a recipe so I can try to make these at home?" Well, I do now, and I'll admit they're pretty darned good. Yup, all gooey outside and crunchy inside. For those times when you can't order 'em, give these a try.

    4 large Red Delicious apples, washed and dried
    1 package (14 ounces) vanilla caramels, unwrapped
    2 tablespoons water
    1 cup (6 ounces) semisweet chocolate chips
    ½ cup slivered almonds, toasted

    4 wooden craft sticks

Line a large rimmed baking sheet with waxed paper and coat with nonstick cooking spray. Insert a wooden craft stick into the stem end of each apple. In a medium saucepan, combine the caramels and water over low heat until melted, stirring constantly. Remove from the heat and spoon over the apples, coating completely. Place the coated apples on the baking sheet and chill for 1 hour. In another medium saucepan, melt the chocolate chips over low heat, stirring constantly. Drizzle over the caramel apples and sprinkle with the nuts. Return to the baking sheet and chill for 30 minutes, or until set.

NOTE
Make these caramel apples your own by covering with your favorite type of chocolate—white, milk, or semisweet, or even using more than one type. And sprinkle with your favorite nuts, sprinkles, or crushed candy. One of my favorites is covered with white chocolate and macadamia nuts.

Death by Chocolate Parfaits

6 servings

As you read earlier in the book, Death by Chocolate is my number-one all-time most-requested recipe . . . but one viewer wrote in with a problem. No, not that it's messy. No, it's certainly not missing any chocolate flavor. The problem is, it's just too large for a small family. The solution? Parfaits in individual-sized servings! With a few conversions and a change here and there, we're in business! That way we can make enough for as many or as few people as we're serving.

6 store-bought or homemade brownies, about 2" × 3"

2 tablespoons coffee-flavored liqueur or strong black coffee

1 package (4-serving size) instant chocolate pudding and pie filling

1½ cups cold milk

1 container (8 ounces) frozen whipped topping, thawed, divided

3 (1.4-ounce) chocolate-covered toffee candy bars, coarsely crushed

Using a fork, prick holes in the top of the brownies. Pour the liqueur over the brownies; let the brownies absorb the liqueur, then crumble. Place half of the crumbled brownies in the bottom of six parfait glasses or dessert dishes. In a medium bowl, combine the chocolate pudding mix and milk; whisk until thickened. Fold in half of the whipped topping; mix well and spoon half of the mixture into the

184

parfait glasses, over the brownies. Top with half of the remaining whipped topping, then half of the crushed candy bars. Repeat the layers once more, ending with the remaining crushed candy bars. Cover and chill for at least 2 hours before serving.

NOTE
Use your favorite brownies in here, and do what's easiest. It doesn't matter whether they're store-bought, made from a mix, or homemade.

DID YOU KNOW . . .

parfait is the French word for perfect? And that's what this dessert is . . . *parfait!*

Wisconsin State Fair Cream Puffs

1 dozen cream puffs

The QVC Local mobile studio is just one of the exciting things to see on the Studio Tour!

I often get letters asking me if I make personal appearances, especially from viewers wanting to know when I'll be in their city. I recently got a similar letter from a viewer in Wisconsin who wanted to know if I had a 50 in 50 Tour like QVC. No, I don't have a tour like that, but I have been known to do quite a bit of traveling during the year. One of my favorite places to visit is the Wisconsin State Fair, 'cause what a fair it is! Can you believe they have a booth that specializes in cream puffs? It's actually more than a booth—it's a whole building! They need it, because these cream puffs are like no others, and people are willing to wait hours for these unique treats. Now I know that there's something special about the fair atmosphere that can't be found any- where else, but at least we can make our own version of the Wisconsin cream puffs so that we don't have to wait till summer and travel to Milwaukee to enjoy these tasty treats.

1 cup water

¼ cup (½ stick) butter, softened

¼ teaspoon salt

1 cup all-purpose flour

4 eggs, at room temperature

1 egg yolk

2 tablespoons milk

2 cups (1 pint) heavy cream

⅓ cup confectioners' sugar, plus extra for sprinkling

2 teaspoons vanilla extract

Preheat the oven to 400°F. In a medium saucepan, bring the water, butter, and salt to a boil over medium-high heat. Add the flour all at once and stir quickly until the mixture forms a ball; remove from the heat. Add 1 egg and beat hard with a wooden spoon to blend. Add the remaining whole eggs one at a time, beating well after each addition; each egg must be completely blended in before the next egg is added. As you beat the mixture, it will change from an almost curdled to a smooth appearance. When it is smooth, spoon twelve mounds of dough onto a large rimmed bak- ing sheet. In a small bowl, combine the egg yolk and milk; mix well and brush over the dough. Bake for 25 to 30 min- utes, or until golden. Remove to a wire rack to cool com- pletely. In a large bowl, beat the cream with an electric

NOTE
For a sure way to get perfect whipped cream, chill the bowl and beaters before whipping the cream, and make sure not to over- beat it.

beater on medium speed until soft peaks form. Add the confectioners' sugar and vanilla and beat until stiff peaks form. Cut the top third off each cooled pastry puff and fill with equal amounts of the whipped cream mixture. Replace the tops and sprinkle with the confectioners' sugar. Serve immediately, or cover and chill until ready to serve.

DID YOU KNOW . . .

thirty-five thousand cream puffs are sold during *each day* of the Wisconsin State Fair?

Home-Smoked Chicken

4 to 6 servings

"Dear Mr. Food: Please help me! My husband loves the flavor of smoked chicken, but with the long winters we have here in Minnesota, unless we shovel a path outside, there's no chicken-smoking for us. Is there any way to get that smoked flavor without using a smoker? Signed, Snowbound in Duluth." Well, Snowbound, here's a secret way for you to enjoy that smoked flavor year-round without shoveling mountains of snow or burning down the house.

One 3- to 3½-pound chicken
1 teaspoon salt
¼ teaspoon black pepper
3 tablespoons liquid smoke

Preheat the oven to 350°F. Place the chicken on a rack in a roasting pan. Rub the chicken with the salt and pepper. Pour the liquid smoke into the bottom of the roasting pan. Cover the pan tightly with aluminum foil and bake for 1 hour. Uncover and bake for 15 to 30 more minutes, or until the juices run clear and no pink remains. Remove the chicken to a serving platter and carve.

DID YOU KNOW . . . even if we buy smoked meats that are not refrigerated, once the packages are opened, they do need to be refrigerated?

NOTE
Heat up some barbecue sauce and serve it on the side for some really good dippin'.

189

Greek Islands Pastitsio

8 to 10 servings

Here's an excerpt from a letter I received: "Dear Mr. Food: I was on a Greek cruise and they served a dish called pastitsio. I loved its creaminess and hearty beef taste, but I wasn't able to get the recipe. Can you please help me so I can make it at home?" As a matter of fact, I can. Here you go, an easy pastitsio recipe to call your very own.

1 pound penne pasta
1 pound ground beef
1 large onion, finely chopped
1 large ripe tomato, chopped
¼ teaspoon ground nutmeg
⅛ teaspoon ground cinnamon
3½ teaspoons salt, divided
1 teaspoon white pepper, divided
1 cup grated Parmesan cheese, divided
½ cup (1 stick) butter
¼ cup all-purpose flour
4 cups milk
4 eggs

Preheat the oven to 375°F. Cook the pasta according to the package directions; drain and set aside. Meanwhile, coat a 9" × 13" baking dish with nonstick cooking spray. In a large skillet, brown the ground beef and onion over high heat for

190

5 minutes, or until no pink remains in the beef, stirring frequently. Add the tomato, nutmeg, cinnamon, 1½ teaspoons salt, and ½ teaspoon pepper. Reduce the heat to medium-low and simmer for 5 to 6 minutes, or until the tomato is soft. Stir in ½ cup cheese, then remove from the heat. Place half of the pasta over the bottom of the baking dish. Spread the meat mixture evenly over the pasta, then top with the remaining pasta; set aside. Melt the butter in a large saucepan over medium-low heat. Add the flour and the remaining 2 teaspoons salt and ½ teaspoon pepper and cook for 3 to 4 minutes, or until lightly browned, stirring constantly. In a medium bowl, combine the milk, eggs, and the remaining ½ cup cheese; mix well. Stir into the flour mixture and cook for 5 to 6 minutes, or until thickened, stirring frequently. Pour evenly over the pasta and bake for 30 to 35 minutes, or until golden and heated through. Serve immediately.

My assistant, Howard Rosenthal, and I always have last-minute details to go over before my shows.

DID YOU KNOW . . . until the mid-nineteenth century, most Americans refused to eat raw tomatoes? They were thought to be toxic!

191

Portobello Wellington

4 servings

DID YOU KNOW . . .

meaty portobello mushrooms are great in salads, tossed with pasta, and even grilled or broiled and served like burgers?

I got e-mail recently asking if I had a recipe for beef Wellington. The viewer said she loves the taste but is trying to cut back on meat. So I went into the kitchen and came up with this version that's pretty darned similar, since portobello mushrooms are so meaty.

> 2 tablespoons butter
> 4 portobello mushroom caps (about 8 ounces total)
> 2 medium onions, chopped
> ½ teaspoon salt
> ¼ teaspoon black pepper
> 1 package (17¼ ounces) frozen puff pastry dough (2 sheets), thawed

NOTE
You can give these extra flavor by serving them with steak sauce on the side.

Preheat the oven to 400°F. Melt the butter in a large skillet over medium-high heat. Add the mushroom caps, onions, salt, and pepper and sauté for 8 to 10 minutes, or until the onions are golden, turning the mushrooms occasionally. On a lightly floured surface, roll out each sheet of pastry with a rolling pin to a 12-inch square. Cut each sheet into four 6-inch squares. Place the mushroom caps on four of the squares. Spoon the onion mixture evenly over the mushroom caps and brush the edges of the pastry with water. Place a second pastry square over each mushroom cap, seal the edges, and crimp with a fork. Place on a large baking sheet and bake for 18 to 20 minutes, or until the pastry is puffed and golden. Serve immediately.

True Blue Cheese Dressing

about 2 cups

My mailbag is always full of surprises! I recently had to solve a family feud where a wife insisted that true Buffalo wings are served with blue cheese dressing while her husband insisted it is ranch dressing. Well, sorry, men, but I have to side with the wife here, because traditional Buffalo-style chicken wings are served with blue cheese dressing. So here it is, my favorite blue cheese dressing recipe. But I have to say that if ranch is your favorite dipping sauce, you should feel free to dip into it to your heart's content.

1½ cups sour cream
¼ cup mayonnaise
1 tablespoon vegetable oil
1 tablespoon white vinegar
1 package (4 ounces) crumbled blue cheese
⅛ teaspoon black pepper
⅛ teaspoon salt (optional)

Place all the ingredients except the salt in a blender. Blend to desired consistency, then add salt, if desired. Serve immediately, or cover and chill until ready to serve.

DID YOU KNOW . . .
Buffalo, New York, claims to be the hometown of spicy, saucy chicken wings? In 1977, they even made July 29 the official "Chicken Wing Day"!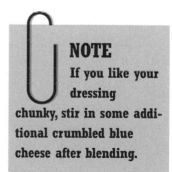

NOTE
If you like your dressing chunky, stir in some additional crumbled blue cheese after blending.

193

Teriyaki Wings

4 to 5 servings

DID YOU KNOW . . .

that in Japanese *teri* means gloss and *yaki* means broiled foods? They make for a great combination whether sweet teriyaki glaze is brushed over foods during the last part of cooking or used in a marinade.

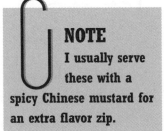

NOTE
I usually serve these with a spicy Chinese mustard for an extra flavor zip.

With Chinese restaurants more popular than ever, everyone is always asking me how to recreate that authentic flavor at home. Well, here's how we can enjoy our favorite appetizer right at home without taking a trip to a specialty store to shop for fancy ingredients.

½ cup soy sauce
⅓ cup firmly packed light brown sugar
1 tablespoon ground ginger
2 teaspoons garlic powder
1 package (5 pounds) frozen chicken wings, thawed

Preheat the oven to 400°F. Line two rimmed baking sheets with aluminum foil, then coat the foil with nonstick cooking spray. In a large bowl, combine all the ingredients except the chicken wings; mix well. Add the chicken wings and toss until evenly coated. Place the chicken wings on the baking sheets, reserving the marinade, and bake for 15 minutes. Meanwhile, place the reserved marinade in a small saucepan and bring to a boil over medium-high heat. Boil for 2 to 3 minutes, or until thickened. Turn the chicken wings over and baste with the marinade. Bake for 15 to 20 minutes, or until no pink remains and the wings are glossy and crisp.

194

Salt-Crusted Chicken

4 to 6 servings

One viewer wrote that one of her fondest memories as a child was the smell of salt-crusted pot roast roasting in the oven. She wanted to know if we could crust other cuts of meat or poultry, and if so, would they taste as good? The answer to both parts of that question is, "You betcha!" I've salted many cuts of beef so this question made me decide to give chicken a try. The most important thing to remember? Make sure the chicken or meat is totally coated, 'cause that's what seals in the flavor and juices. And when it's cooked, we simply crack off the crust and enjoy.

4 cups kosher (coarse) salt
1 cup water
1 tablespoon honey
1 tablespoon spicy brown mustard
One 3- to 3½-pound chicken

Preheat the oven to 450°F. Line a roasting pan with aluminum foil. In a large bowl, combine the salt and water; mix well. Place half of the mixture in the center of the roasting pan. In a small bowl, combine the honey and mustard; rub evenly over the chicken. Place the chicken in the roasting pan over the salt mixture, then coat with the remaining salt mixture, completely patting the mixture over the chicken and forming a crust. Bake for 1¼ to 1½ hours, or until the juices run clear and no pink remains. Carefully remove the salt crust (it'll be hot!) and serve the chicken.

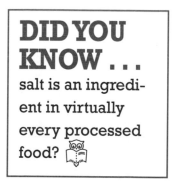

DID YOU KNOW . . .
salt is an ingredient in virtually every processed food?

195

Chip 'n' Dip Chicken

4 to 6 servings

DID YOU KNOW . . . the first flavored potato chips were produced in the late 1940s? Guess what flavor they were: Barbecue! Sour cream and onion was next.

Kids can be some of the most finicky eaters around and one of my viewers wrote in and told me she had a couple of young ones who only wanted to eat chips and dip. No matter what she made, that's all they would eat—they were practically addicted. So I created a special recipe—chip 'n' dip chicken—that combined their favorite tastes with chicken, so at least they'd get *something* else to eat!

½ cup ranch salad dressing
1 teaspoon garlic powder
¼ teaspoon ground red pepper
1 package (6 ounces) sour cream and onion potato chips, crushed
One 3- to 3½-pound chicken, cut into 8 pieces

Preheat the oven to 400°F. Coat a large rimmed baking sheet with nonstick cooking spray. In a shallow bowl, combine the dressing, garlic powder, and red pepper; mix well. Place the crushed potato chips in another shallow bowl. Dip the chicken pieces in the dressing mixture, then in the crushed potato chips, coating completely. Place on the baking sheet and bake for 35 to 40 minutes, or until no pink remains.

NOTE For extra flavor, drizzle the chicken with additional ranch dressing before serving.

Crispy Coconut Shrimp

Orange-Glazed
Cornish Hens

Sautéed
Brussels Sprouts

Zucchini
Wild Rice

J

Bob Bowersox
Sweet-and-Sour Chicken

K

Garlicky
Breadsticks

Lisa Mason's
Vegetable Lasagna

L

from the Kitchen of:
LISA MASON
VEGETABLE LASAGNA

9 lasagna noodles
2 tablespoons vegetable
2 yellow squash -
½-inch-thi
1 medium

Spicy Meaty Quiche

6 to 8 servings

I was in a bookstore signing some cookbooks when a young lady brought over the book *Real Men Don't Eat Quiche* and asked my opinion of the title. "Yup, they sure do!" I told her. After all, it's just a cheesy pie. As a matter of fact, both sexes will be lining up for this quiche that's flavor-packed, meaty, and extra cheesy.

½ pound pepper-Jack cheese, shredded
One 9-inch frozen ready-to-bake deep-dish pie shell, thawed
½ pound sliced deli roast beef, chopped
1 cup (½ pint) heavy cream
4 eggs
¼ teaspoon dry mustard
¼ teaspoon black pepper

Preheat the oven to 325°F. Sprinkle half of the cheese evenly over the bottom of the pie shell; top with the roast beef, then with the remaining cheese. In a medium bowl, whisk together the remaining ingredients; pour over the cheese. Bake for 55 to 60 minutes, or until a knife inserted in the center comes out clean. Serve immediately.

DID YOU KNOW . . .

the first quiche to become popular in the United States was quiche lorraine? It's an egg, onion, cheese, and bacon pie. Today, we see quiches made with everything from veggies and cheese to sausage and peppers.

NOTE

For a spicier quiche, add some chopped fresh jalapeños to the cream mixture.

197

Smothered Chicken

4 to 6 servings

Every week when the mail comes in, there always seems to be a fair amount of requests for this recipe or that recipe that somebody's grandma used to make. So often I hear about how Grandma was a great cook who rarely wrote down her recipes. Recently, a family from Arkansas asked me if I had a recipe for what they grew up calling Smothered Chicken. I had to do a bit of searching before I found a version that I then simplified. And you know what? Now it's easy enough for any busy night of the week . . . you'll see.

½ cup all-purpose flour
1 teaspoon salt
1¼ teaspoons black pepper
One 3- to 3½-pound chicken, cut into 8 pieces and rinsed (not dried)
⅓ cup vegetable oil
4 medium onions, thinly sliced
1 pound fresh mushrooms, sliced
2 cans (10¾ ounces each) condensed cream of mushroom soup
½ cup rosé wine

In a shallow dish, combine the flour, salt, and pepper; mix well. Dip the chicken in the flour mixture, coating well. In

a soup pot, heat the oil over medium heat. Cook the coated chicken in batches for 4 to 5 minutes per side, until browned. Drain on a paper towel–lined platter. Add the onions and mushrooms to the pot and sauté for 5 minutes. Return the chicken to the pot and stir in the soup and wine. Reduce the heat to medium-low, cover, and simmer for 55 to 60 minutes, or until the chicken is tender and no pink remains, stirring occasionally.

NOTE
Why not make this a complete meal by serving it over cooked rice or curly noodles?

DID YOU KNOW . . .

to get thick soup to come out of the can easily you just have to shake it up a bit first? Then open it from the bottom—it should slide right out!

Welsh Rabbit

about 2 cups

NOTE
Traditionally this is served over toast points and topped with sliced tomatoes, crumbled bacon, and sliced scallions, but you can also use it as you would any other cheese sauce.

Recently I opened a letter with a request for rabbit recipes, "maybe like Welsh Rabbit or any other ones." My response? No, I don't have any rabbit recipes. (And if you know what Welsh Rabbit is, you've gotta laugh, since there isn't even any rabbit in it!) But I do have this recipe for Welsh Rabbit, also known as Welsh Rarebit. Hoppy eating!

3 cups (12 ounces) shredded sharp Cheddar cheese
¾ cup milk
2 teaspoons Worcestershire sauce
1½ teaspoons dry mustard
¼ teaspoon ground red pepper
1 egg, beaten

In a medium saucepan, combine all the ingredients except the egg over medium-low heat; mix well. Stir in the egg and heat until the cheese has melted and the mixture has thickened. Serve immediately.

DID YOU KNOW . . .
Welsh rabbit is what rabbit hunters had to eat when they returned home from the hunt empty-handed?!

Sweet-and-Sour Coleslaw

6 to 8 servings

During the summer, we always make lots of salads, and it seems like most of them are made with mayonnaise. Well, sometimes we want a salad that tastes a little bit different. So this coleslaw, made with a vinegar base, that was sent in by a viewer, is the perfect change-of-pace answer. I promise you won't miss the mayo.

¼ cup (½ stick) butter

¾ cup cider vinegar

½ cup sugar

2 tablespoons all-purpose flour

1 teaspoon dry mustard

¼ teaspoon garlic powder

1 teaspoon salt

½ teaspoon black pepper

1 egg, lightly beaten

2 packages (16 ounces each) coleslaw mix

In a medium saucepan, melt the butter over medium heat. Add the vinegar, sugar, flour, mustard, garlic powder, salt, and pepper; whisk until well combined. Slowly whisk in the egg. Cook for 1 to 2 minutes, or until the mixture has thickened, whisking constantly. Remove from the heat and allow to cool slightly. In a large bowl, combine the coleslaw mix and the vinegar mixture; toss until well coated. Serve, or cover and chill until ready to serve.

DID YOU KNOW . . . sweet pickle juice can be used in place of vinegar when we want to sweeten our coleslaw and give it a different flavor?

NOTE
This can also be made with fresh cabbage. Just shred a medium head of green cabbage and half a head of red cabbage. I also like to add some shredded carrot for color.

201

Quick 'n' Easy Beef Stroganoff

4 servings

 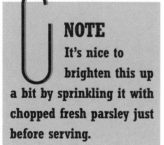
Many of my viewers write in to share their suggestions for how to make our favorite meals a little quicker and maybe a little easier, too. Here's one of my favorites—a beef stroganoff that's ready in under thirty minutes. Aren't you glad we shared?

1 package (8 ounces) egg noodles
2 cans (12 ounces each) roast beef chunks with gravy, drained
1 small onion, diced
1 can (10¾ ounces) condensed cream of mushroom soup
1 cup sour cream
½ teaspoon garlic powder

NOTE
It's nice to brighten this up a bit by sprinkling it with chopped fresh parsley just before serving.

Cook the noodles according to the package directions; drain and keep warm. Meanwhile, in a large skillet, cook the roast beef and onion over medium-high heat for 4 to 5 minutes, or until the onion is tender, stirring constantly. Stir in the remaining ingredients except the noodles. Reduce the heat to medium and cook for 5 to 6 minutes, or until heated through. Serve over the noodles.

Veggie-Packed Chili

6 to 8 servings

A hearty beef chili is a staple in most households, but every once in a while we crave something a little different— maybe a little lighter or a little spicier, but still full of that chili flavor we love. So why not try this veggie-packed chili recipe that a viewer from California shared? It's tasty and good for us, too!

1 tablespoon olive oil

1 large onion, chopped

1 can (28 ounces) crushed tomatoes

⅔ cup salsa (see Note)

1½ teaspoons chili powder

1½ teaspoons ground cumin

¾ teaspoon salt

2 cans (15 ounces each) black beans, rinsed and drained

1 large red bell pepper, cut into ½-inch chunks

1 large zucchini, cut into ½-inch chunks

1 medium yellow squash, cut into ½-inch chunks

In a soup pot, heat the oil over medium heat. Add the onion and sauté for 2 to 3 minutes, or until tender. Add the tomatoes, salsa, chili powder, cumin, and salt; mix well. Reduce the heat to low, cover, and simmer for 10 minutes. Add the remaining ingredients, cover, and simmer for 50 to 60 minutes, or until the vegetables are tender.

DID YOU KNOW . . .
we can add fresh flavor by using Ron Maestri's homemade salsa (page 36) in here?

NOTE
In this dish, we'll get most of the kick from the salsa, so whichever intensity you use—from mild to hot—is your choice.

Eggplant Lasagna

6 to 8 servings

Mamma mia! A young bride wrote to me, pleading for an eggplant lasagna recipe that she could make for her in-laws, since she knew it was their favorite dish. I sent her this recipe and wished her luck. A few months later, I got a note from the newlyweds asking for a good dessert recipe. The lasagna had been a big hit, but her dessert had flopped. Oh, well, she gets an A for effort!

> 2 medium eggplant, peeled and thinly sliced (see Note)
> 8 cups water
> 2 tablespoons salt
> 1 jar (28 ounces) spaghetti sauce
> 1 container (15 ounces) ricotta cheese
> ¼ teaspoon black pepper
> 3 cups (12 ounces) shredded mozzarella cheese

Preheat the oven to 375°F. In a large bowl, combine the eggplant slices, water, and the salt; soak for 30 minutes. Drain the eggplant and place on paper towels to dry. Coat a 9" × 13" baking dish with nonstick cooking spray. Pour half the spaghetti sauce over the bottom of the baking dish. In a small bowl, combine the ricotta cheese and pepper; mix well. Layer one quarter of the eggplant slices over the sauce, then top with one third of the ricotta cheese mixture and ¾ cup mozzarella cheese. Repeat the eggplant, ricotta, and mozzarella layers two more times. Top with the remaining eggplant and spread the remaining sauce over the top. Cover with aluminum foil and bake for 1 hour. Sprinkle with the remaining ¾ cup mozzarella cheese and bake, uncovered, for 15 to 20 minutes, or until the cheese has melted and the eggplant is tender.

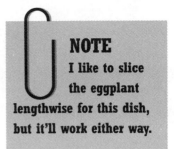

NOTE
I like to slice the eggplant lengthwise for this dish, but it'll work either way.

DID YOU KNOW . . .

eggplant is seed-bearing, so it falls into the category of "fruit-vegetable," along with squash, peppers, and tomatoes?

Mashed Sweet Potatoes

6 to 8 servings

A viewer wrote and said he was tired of always eating his sweet potatoes the same way—simply baked. He wanted to know if there was a new way to try 'em. Guess what?! Sweet potatoes can be prepared almost any way that regular potatoes are. And this mashed version is all the proof we need.

> 6 medium sweet potatoes (about 3 pounds), peeled and quartered
> ½ cup (1 stick) butter, softened
> ½ cup milk
> ¼ teaspoon garlic powder
> ¾ teaspoon salt
> ½ teaspoon black pepper

NOTE
For a special finishing touch, and to add just a bit of sweetness, drizzle with honey and sprinkle with cinnamon.

Place the potatoes in a soup pot and add just enough water to cover them. Bring to a boil over medium-high heat. Reduce the heat to medium-low, cover, and cook for 15 to 20 minutes, or until fork-tender; drain. In a large bowl, combine the potatoes with the remaining ingredients and beat with an electric beater on medium speed for 2 to 3 minutes, or until smooth. Serve immediately.

Pecan-Smoked Chicken

6 servings

One of my Southern viewers sent me this idea and I'll admit that at first I was a little hesitant. I mean, I had never heard of smoking a chicken with pecan shells. But once I tried it, I changed my mind, and y'all will, too.

2 cups pecan shells

4 cups water

2 tablespoons vegetable oil

1 tablespoon dried rosemary

½ teaspoon salt

½ teaspoon black pepper

6 boneless, skinless chicken breast halves (1½ to 2 pounds total)

Preheat the grill to medium heat. In a medium bowl, combine the pecan shells and the water; soak for 15 minutes. Drain and place over the coals of the barbecue grill (see Note). Cover the grill and allow to heat for 5 minutes. Meanwhile, in a small bowl, combine the oil, rosemary, salt, and pepper; mix well and brush over both sides of the chicken breasts. Grill, covered, for 4 to 5 minutes per side, or until no pink remains. Serve immediately.

DID YOU KNOW . . . after the peanut, the pecan is the second favorite nut grown in the United States?

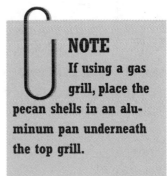

NOTE
If using a gas grill, place the pecan shells in an aluminum pan underneath the top grill.

Asparagus Muffins

1 dozen muffins

DID YOU KNOW . . .

we can add fiber to our diets by sprinkling a bit of oatmeal on any of our muffins before baking?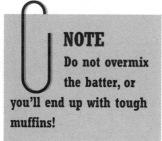

Afternoon tea is a tradition in many of the Southern states that I visit. Once, while I was having tea with some friends in Georgia, we all began discussing the different ways Southerners prepare muffins, and there were just so many! Wouldn't you know it—a few weeks later I received a whole bunch of muffin recipes, including this unusual one.

2 cups biscuit baking mix
⅔ cup milk
1 egg
¾ cup (3 ounces) shredded mozzarella cheese
1 can (15 ounces) asparagus spears, drained and cut into ½-inch pieces

NOTE
Do not overmix the batter, or you'll end up with tough muffins!

Preheat the oven to 400°F. Coat a 12-cup muffin tin with nonstick cooking spray. In a medium bowl, combine the baking mix, milk, and egg; mix well. Stir in the cheese and asparagus until well combined. Spoon into the muffin cups and bake for 15 to 18 minutes, or until golden and a wooden toothpick inserted in the center comes out clean. Serve warm.

Party Pizza Spread

10 to 12 servings

My TV station in Cape Girardeau, Missouri, had a recipe contest and the winner received an autographed copy of *Mr. Food®'s EasyCooking* magazine. There were so many good entries and, to me, they were all winners. But this one really was outstanding, and kind of unusual 'cause there's no cooking involved at all, so I wanted to share it with you.

1 package (8 ounces) cream cheese, softened
½ cup sour cream
½ teaspoon onion powder
¼ teaspoon garlic powder
¾ cup pizza or spaghetti sauce
1 package (3½ ounces) sliced pepperoni, chopped
1 jar (6 ounces) sliced mushrooms, drained
1 cup (4 ounces) shredded mozzarella cheese
2 scallions, thinly sliced
1 can (2¼ ounces) sliced black olives, drained

In a medium bowl, with an electric beater on medium speed, beat the cream cheese, sour cream, onion powder, and garlic powder until smooth. Spread evenly over the bottom of a 9-inch pie plate. Spread the pizza sauce over it, then layer the pepperoni, mushrooms, cheese, scallions, and olives over the sauce. Serve immediately.

DID YOU KNOW . . . it's easy to fancy up the ice cubes for our parties? We can just add olives, maraschino cherries, or cocktail onions to the filled ice cube tray before freezing.

NOTE Serve this as a spread with crackers or thin slices of Italian bread. And, if you prefer, it can also be served warm. Just heat it in a 325°F. oven for 10 minutes before serving.

Lemon-Parmesan Bread

14 to 16 slices

A Florida viewer sent me this "twist" on an old favorite recipe. She has a lemon tree growing right in her backyard, so she takes advantage of it and uses lots of lemons in her cooking. It's fun to add them to our standard recipes to give them a refreshing zing.

⅓ cup grated Parmesan cheese
¼ cup (½ stick) butter, melted
1 lemon, peeled, sectioned, and finely chopped
1 loaf (16 ounces) Italian bread, cut into 1-inch slices

Preheat the broiler. In a small bowl, combine the cheese, butter, and lemon; mix well. Brush the top of each bread slice with the mixture. Place on a large rimmed baking sheet. Broil for 1 to 2 minutes, or until lightly browned. Serve warm.

NOTE For some added color, add some chopped fresh parsley to the cheese mixture before brushing it on the bread.

Roasted Pumpkin

8 servings

Yes, yes, yes! That's the answer to all those folks who wrote to me this past year, asking if they can cook fresh pumpkins. Pumpkins are really just another variety of squash and can be roasted or boiled, just like any of their "cousins."

One 3-pound pumpkin, washed, seeds and strings removed, hollowed, and cut into 2-inch chunks (see Note)
2 tablespoons butter, melted
½ teaspoon salt
½ teaspoon black pepper

Preheat the oven to 450°F. Coat a large rimmed baking sheet with nonstick cooking spray. In a large bowl, combine all the ingredients; toss to coat well. Spread the chunks on the baking sheet and roast for 30 to 35 minutes, or until fork-tender. Serve immediately.

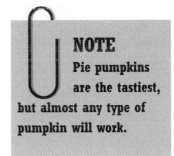

NOTE
Pie pumpkins are the tastiest, but almost any type of pumpkin will work.

DID YOU KNOW . . .

we shouldn't eat any pumpkins we've used as jack-o'-lanterns, or ones that we've painted or decorated or burned a candle in?

Old-fashioned Creamed Tuna

about 4 servings

Spices sure can be confusing. Why? All it takes is an afternoon browsing through my mail to see that. One viewer asked why five-spice powder is called that if the list of ingredients in various brands shows seven to ten spices in the blend. Good question. But I'd say that, from all my letters, nutmeg is the most asked about; people aren't really sure how to use it. Now for some answers: Five-spice powder did originally contain just five spices, hence its name. And as for nutmeg, I think it's best when we add a little to creamy sauces or cheese dishes like this tuna. Why not try a dash of nutmeg every once in a while in your cooking? Experimenting with new flavors and combinations is a great way to expand your taste buds.

¼ cup (½ stick) butter
1 small onion, finely chopped
¼ cup all-purpose flour
¼ teaspoon ground nutmeg
½ teaspoon salt
¼ teaspoon black pepper
2 cups milk
1 can (12 ounces) tuna, drained and flaked
1 package (10 ounces) frozen peas, thawed (optional)
½ cup sour cream

In a large saucepan, melt the butter over medium heat. Add the onion and sauté for 2 to 3 minutes, or until tender. Add the flour, nutmeg, salt, and pepper; sauté for 1 minute. Gradually stir in the milk and bring to a boil. Reduce the heat to medium-low and simmer for 2 to 3 minutes, or until thickened, stirring constantly. Stir in the tuna, peas (if desired), and sour cream and cook just until heated through. Serve immediately.

NOTE
How elegant this can be served over toast points or buttered noodles.

DID YOU KNOW . . .

tuna is such a versatile fish that it can be baked, braised, broiled, grilled, sautéed, or even stewed? It's also popular these days eaten raw in sushi.

Almond-Crusted Flounder

4 servings

"Dear Mr. Food: I live on Long Island and I watch you on WABC-TV. Since we live near the ocean, every summer we go fishing and bring in lots of flounder. Do you have any new recipes that will work well with this delicate fish?" Oh, I love fresh fish and flounder is great simply sautéed with butter and lemon. But for a change of pace, try this almond-crusted version that I got from my fishing buddies in Rhode Island. Enjoy!

1 tablespoon sugar
¾ teaspoon ground cinnamon
¼ teaspoon ground red pepper
½ teaspoon salt
1½ pounds flounder fillets
1 egg white, beaten
2 cups sliced almonds
2 tablespoons butter, plus more as needed
¼ cup olive oil, plus more as needed
½ cup amaretto liqueur

In a small bowl, combine the sugar, cinnamon, red pepper, and salt; mix well. Season the fillets with 1 teaspoon of the mixture, reserving the remaining mixture. Place the egg white in a shallow dish; place the almonds in another shallow dish. Dip each fillet into the egg white, then into the almonds, coating completely. In a large skillet, melt the butter with the oil over medium heat. Add half of the fillets and cook for 5 minutes, then turn and cook for 2 to 3 more minutes, or until the fish flakes easily with a fork; transfer to a serving platter and cover to keep warm. Repeat with the remaining fillets, adding additional butter and oil as needed. Add the reserved sugar mixture and the amaretto to the skillet; reduce the heat to low and cook for 1 to 2 minutes, or until thickened, stirring constantly. Pour over the fillets and serve immediately.

DID YOU KNOW . . .

spices shouldn't be stored over the oven or near an exhaust fan, because heat makes 'em dry up and lose flavor?

Spanish Orzo

4 to 6 servings

Many years ago, in my *Quick and Easy Side Dishes* book, I made a recipe called Mushroom Charlotte, which calls for orzo or rosamarina pasta. I have to say it was a super recipe. About four months ago I got a letter from a viewer telling me how popular this side dish is at her house. She said that everybody thinks the orzo is really plump rice! She asked me if I had any other recipes that use orzo and, guess what?! Yes, I do! However, you can cook it up and use it as you would cooked rice in many recipes. Try it in this Spanish rice makeover.

> 1 package (16 ounces) orzo (rosamarina) pasta
> 2 tablespoons olive oil
> 1 pound ground beef
> ½ pound fresh mushrooms, coarsely chopped
> 1 medium onion, chopped
> 1½ teaspoons garlic powder
> ½ teaspoon black pepper
> 1 jar (28 ounces) spaghetti sauce
> 1 cup salsa (see Note)

Cook the orzo according to the package directions; drain. Heat the oil in a large skillet over high heat. Add the beef, mushrooms, onion, garlic powder, and pepper and cook for 8 to 10 minutes, or until the vegetables are tender and the beef is no longer pink, stirring frequently. Add the orzo, spaghetti sauce, and salsa. Reduce the heat to low and cook for 3 to 5 minutes, or until heated through, stirring frequently.

NOTE
Orzo is great for adding to soups to make them extra-hearty.

DID YOU KNOW . . .
the average American eats over nineteen pounds of pasta annually?

Zucchini Wild Rice

4 to 6 servings

DID YOU KNOW . . .
Minute Rice®, the first precooked rice that could be cooked at home in under ten minutes, was introduced in 1949?

A young man e-mailed me and said that he had recently married and that he and his wife share the cooking responsibilities at their house. He always makes noodles as a side dish, 'cause they're her favorite. And on her nights to cook, she makes him wild rice. One night, he mixed together their side dish leftovers and came up with this great combo that he shared with me. You know, I've always said that some of the best recipes happen by accident, and it's true here, too.

3 tablespoons vegetable oil
1 large zucchini, cut into ½-inch chunks
1 medium onion, chopped
2 cups uncooked fine egg noodles
2 cans (14½ ounces each) ready-to-use chicken broth
1 package (6 ounces) long-grain and wild rice mix with seasoning packet

NOTE
I use zucchini in this version, but just about any fresh vegetable can be chopped and added to the dish, depending upon what you have in the veggie bin.

Heat the oil in a large skillet over medium-high heat. Add the zucchini and onion and sauté for 6 to 8 minutes, or until lightly browned. Add the noodles and cook for 4 to 6 minutes, or until browned, stirring occasionally. Add the remaining ingredients; mix well and bring to a boil. Reduce the heat to low, cover, and cook for 20 to 25 minutes, or until all the liquid is absorbed.

Sautéed Brussels Sprouts

4 to 6 servings

The mail comes in from all over the country, from every age from kids to great-grandparents. One day, I got a letter from an elementary school class asking me a bunch of food questions. One of them was, "Do you know how Brussels sprouts grow?" I thought that was an interesting question for a first-grader. The answer? They grow straight up in the air on stalks about two feet long. The cabbage-like sprouts look like miniature ornaments on a Christmas tree. If you'd like to find the fresh sprouts still on the stalk, ask your supermarket produce manager to get them for you as a special treat.

DID YOU KNOW . . . Brussels sprouts are a member of the cabbage family and have a sweet, nutty flavor?

¼ cup (½ stick) butter

1 medium onion, thinly sliced

2 packages (10 ounces each) frozen Brussels sprouts, thawed

½ teaspoon ground nutmeg

¼ teaspoon salt

¼ teaspoon black pepper

Melt the butter in a large skillet over medium heat. Add the onion and sauté for 1 to 2 minutes, or until tender. Stir in the remaining ingredients and sauté for 5 to 7 minutes, or until heated through. Serve immediately.

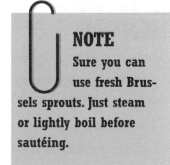

NOTE Sure you can use fresh Brussels sprouts. Just steam or lightly boil before sautéing.

Quick Apple Crisp

4 to 6 servings

NOTE
This is a no-fuss dessert that can't be beat—especially when you serve it topped with a scoop of vanilla ice cream. And why not be adventurous and try it with peach, cherry, blueberry, or any other favorite pie filling flavor?

My mail shows me that people are always looking for short-cuts and, thankfully, they're willing to share recipes as well. This recipe came to me from a busy mom whose kids love apple crisp. One day she tried this quick version and it was a smash hit!

1 can (21 ounces) apple pie filling
2 cups granola cereal
½ cup (1 stick) butter, melted

Preheat the oven to 375°F. Spread the pie filling over the bottom of an 8-inch square baking dish. In a small bowl, combine the cereal and butter; mix well. Sprinkle over the pie filling and bake for 20 to 25 minutes, or until heated through.

DID YOU KNOW . . .
ripe apples should always be stored in the refrigerator? They spoil much faster at room temperature.

Ordering on-line from iQVC sure is easy . . . and I'm no computer whiz!

Foods to Go

One of the best ways to tell someone that you really care is with food. It could be as simple as baking a batch of cookies to take to a neighbor or shipping a favorite old family recipe to someone to say, "I love you." But often we don't know what to ship to that special person. So here's an entire chapter of yummy goodies that travel well. Whether they're going down the block or across the country, these items will travel especially well. I even picked up a few tips from watching the folks in the mailroom at QVC. Boy, do they know how to pack! As a matter of fact, each product goes through numerous quality assurance steps to be sure our purchases arrive safe and sound on our doorsteps. Give these recipes a shot and test out all we've learned . . . while sending a hug to a loved one far away or right next door.

Foods to Go

*Q is for Quality, A is for Assurance—
and that's what QVC's all about.*

Cinnamon Coffee Mix

**3½ cups mix,
14 servings**

For the java connoisseur, here's a special blend of brew we can create with just a few ingredients. Package it in a decorative container, a colorful mug, or gift bag for an anytime gift by itself, or make it even more special by tucking in a package or two of Chocolate Chip Biscotti (page 226) and Jelly Bean Brittle (page 238). It's sure to bring out the biggest grin possible.

2 cups powdered nondairy creamer
1 cup instant coffee granules
1 cup sugar
1 tablespoon ground cinnamon

In a blender, blend all the ingredients on high speed for 1 minute, or until well combined. Store in an airtight container.

NOTE
Don't forget to add a note saying how to make Cinnamon Coffee. Here's how: Stir ¼ cup of this mix into 1 cup of boiling water until dissolved, and enjoy!

DID YOU KNOW . . .

an easy way to make flavored coffee is to pour ground coffee into the filter, then sprinkle some cinnamon on top before brewing?

Chocolate-Studded Banana Bread

6 mini loaves

Have a few wide-mouthed canning jars on hand? Put them to good use with this banana bread that's filled with lots of little surprises. Why, the breads are baked right in the jar! So wrap some ribbon around the lid or maybe tie it in a bow and . . . ta da! Now pop it in a box with some packing peanuts and off it goes. It's the perfect gift that's easy to ship, 'cause the jar keeps it fresh and protects it from being crushed.

½ cup (1 stick) butter, softened
1¼ cups sugar
2 eggs
3 ripe bananas
2½ cups all-purpose flour
1 teaspoon baking soda
1 teaspoon vanilla extract
¾ cup milk chocolate chips

Six wide-mouthed 1-pint canning jars

Preheat the oven to 350°F. In a large bowl, with an electric beater on medium speed, beat the butter, sugar, eggs, and bananas until well combined. Stir in the flour, baking soda, and vanilla; mix well (the batter will be stiff). Stir in the chocolate chips until well combined. Spoon the batter into the six jars. Place the jars on a baking sheet. Bake, uncovered, for 35 to 40 minutes, or until a wooden toothpick inserted in the center comes out clean. Remove from the oven and immediately seal each jar. Allow to cool completely at room temperature. When ready to serve, remove from the jars and slice.

NOTE
It's nice to give these an extra homey touch by decorating each with a small piece of pretty cloth placed over the lid and tied with a ribbon.

DID YOU KNOW ...

chocolate chip cookies were created in the 1930s by Ruth Wakefield, proprietress of the Toll House Inn? She was expecting the bits of chocolate that she added to her cookies to melt, but they didn't ... and the rest is history!

Chocolate Chip Biscotti

about 4 dozen

When my kids were away at college, I liked sending them care packages full of chocolate chip cookies and other goodies. But it seems that by the time the cookies arrived, there often was nothing left but a big box of crumbs. What did I finally do? Simple! I invented this recipe for the durable chocolate chip delight . . . biscotti. Ever seen 'em? Look on color page N. They're perfect for shipping off to friends when they need some cheering up. How about including a note saying something like "Here's a little something to brighten your day."

> 3 cups all-purpose flour
> 2 cups sugar
> ½ teaspoon salt
> 1 teaspoon baking powder
> 4 eggs
> 1 teaspoon vanilla extract
> 1 cup (6 ounces) mini semisweet chocolate chips

Preheat the oven to 350°F. Coat two large cookie sheets with nonstick cooking spray. In a large bowl, combine all the ingredients except the chocolate chips; mix well. Stir in the chocolate chips. Place half of the dough on one cookie sheet; form into a 3" × 12" loaf about 1 inch high. Repeat with the remaining dough on the second cookie sheet.

Bake for 25 to 30 minutes, or until firm and light golden. Remove from the oven and reduce the heat to 325°F. Allow the loaves to cool for 5 minutes. Cut into ½-inch slices and place on the cookie sheets, cut side down. Bake for 15 minutes, then turn over and bake for 15 more minutes, or until very crisp. Allow to cool, then store in an airtight container.

DID YOU KNOW . . .

if chocolate is stored under damp, cold conditions, its surface often turns gray? Don't worry! It shouldn't affect the chocolate's taste or quality.

NOTE
For Chocolate Chocolate Chip Biscotti, replace ½ cup of the flour with ½ cup unsweetened cocoa and proceed as directed.

227

Traditional Chicken Soup

6 to 8 servings

At one time or another, we've all had a friend or family member who felt a little under the weather. As the old saying goes, chicken soup is the best medicine—and I can't think of anyone who didn't want a steaming bowl of chicken soup to help make them feel better. So why not make a batch, cool it, and place it in a container to be delivered in person. Or you can always freeze it in a tightly sealed plastic container (no more than two thirds full) till it's rock-solid, place the container in a plastic bag with a cold pack or two, and ship it overnight packed in packing peanuts or newspaper in a disposable Styrofoam cooler. Can you think of a better way to make someone feel better?

One 3- to 3½-pound chicken
3 carrots, cut into 1-inch pieces
3 celery stalks, cut into 1-inch pieces
1 medium onion, quartered
8 cups water
2½ teaspoons salt
½ teaspoon black pepper

In a soup pot, combine all the ingredients and bring to a boil over high heat. Reduce the heat to medium-low, cover, and simmer for 2½ to 3 hours, or until the chicken easily falls off the bones. Remove the chicken from the pot. Allow the chicken to cool slightly, then remove the skin and bones and cut the meat into bite-sized pieces; discard the skin and bones. Return the chicken pieces to the pot and cook over medium heat until heated through.

NOTE
For chicken noodle soup, add 2 to 3 cups cooked egg noodles to the soup; and for chicken-rice soup, add 2 to 3 cups cooked rice.

DID YOU KNOW . . .

carrots shouldn't be stored with apples? That's because apples emit a gas which can make the carrots taste bitter.

It's a few minutes till showtime and Video Production Supervisor Carol Hirko and I say a quick hello.

Maple Walnut Fudge

about 5 dozen pieces

Since I haven't had an old-time candy shop in my neighborhood for years, I'd gotten used to ordering fudge through the mail. But by the time it arrived at my house, it was often melted and out of shape. So I created my own fudge that not only ships well but tastes incredible. A box of this shipped to a friend says that even though you might be miles apart, you're still close by.

½ cup (1 stick) butter
½ cup heavy cream
½ cup granulated sugar
½ cup firmly packed light brown sugar
⅛ teaspoon salt
1 cup chopped walnuts
2 teaspoons maple flavor
2 cups confectioners' sugar

Coat an 8-inch square baking dish with nonstick cooking spray. In a large saucepan, bring the butter, heavy cream, granulated sugar, brown sugar, and salt to a boil over medium heat, stirring frequently. Boil for 5 minutes, stirring constantly. Remove from the heat and stir in the walnuts and maple flavor. Stir in the confectioners' sugar until smooth and well combined. Spread evenly in the baking dish. Cool to room temperature. Cut into 1-inch squares and serve, or store in an airtight container.

DID YOU KNOW . . .

there are loads of different fudge flavors? Just about every flavor from raspberry to peanut butter can be found at most candy stores.

Toffee Almond Popcorn

about 10 cups

One of the best things to ship is popcorn. As a matter of fact, you can use popcorn to protect cookies when you ship them. So here's a dressed-up popcorn that's perfect for shipping . . . all by itself!

    10 cups popped popcorn
    1 cup roasted almonds
    1 package (7½ ounces) almond brickle chips
    ½ cup light corn syrup

Preheat the oven to 275°F. Coat two large rimmed baking sheets with nonstick cooking spray. In a large bowl, combine the popcorn and almonds; mix well and divide evenly between the baking sheets. In a medium saucepan, combine the brickle chips and corn syrup over medium heat for 10 to 12 minutes, or until the chips are melted, stirring constantly. Pour evenly over the popcorn and almonds and stir to mix well. Bake for 25 to 30 minutes, or until golden, stirring every 10 minutes. Remove from the oven and allow to cool completely, stirring every few minutes. Break up any large pieces and store in an airtight container.

DID YOU KNOW . . . popcorn was served at the very first Thanksgiving dinner?

Cinnamon Swirl Coffee Can Cake

2 loaves, 12 to 16 slices in all

During the holidays it's easy to forget and leave a few people off our lists . . . especially with everything that we have going on. So I always bake a few of these cakes to have on hand just in case. I like to wrap 'em in colored plastic wrap. That way they make great take-along treats for the hairdresser, teachers, and any last-minute "thank-yous" at holiday time.

> 1¼ cups plus 1 tablespoon sugar, divided
> ¼ cup (½ stick) butter, softened
> 1 egg
> 2 cups all-purpose flour
> 1 teaspoon baking soda
> 1 cup water
> ½ teaspoon vanilla extract
> ½ cup chopped walnuts
> 1 teaspoon ground cinnamon

Preheat the oven to 350°F. Coat two clean 12- to 15-ounce coffee cans with nonstick cooking spray. In a large bowl, with an electric beater on low speed, cream together 1¼ cups sugar and the butter. Add the egg; blend well. Beat in the flour and baking soda until well combined. Beat in the water and vanilla until smooth. Stir in the walnuts; mix well. Place 1 cup of the batter in a small bowl and add the remaining 1 tablespoon sugar and the cinnamon; mix well. Divide half of the plain batter equally between the coffee cans, then top with equal amounts of cinnamon batter. Top with the remaining plain batter. Using a knife, swirl the batters together. Place both cans on a baking sheet and bake for 50 to 55 minutes, or until a wooden toothpick inserted in the center comes out clean. Allow to cool for 15 minutes, then remove from the cans to cool completely. Slice and serve.

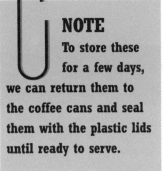

NOTE
To store these for a few days, we can return them to the coffee cans and seal them with the plastic lids until ready to serve.

DID YOU KNOW . . .

the wrapper from a stick of butter or margarine can come in handy for greasing baking pans?

Country Apple Rings

about 30 rings

Apple picking is so much fun! There are so many apples, and so few weekends to go picking! When we used to go with the kids, we always ended up with way more apples than we could eat in just a few weeks and, besides, the apples start getting soft before long. Well, now I've got a good idea for a homey apple treat that just takes a little slicing and some slow oven-drying. Whether we eat them ourselves or pack 'em for a friend who may not be able to get fresh-picked apples, these dried apple rings will last a long time. And if we ship them, it's nice to toss a few dried maple leaves into the box to add a touch of autumn.

4 apples, cored and cut crosswise into ¼-inch slices
2 cups lemon juice
2 teaspoons salt

Preheat the oven to 200°F. In a large resealable plastic storage bag, combine all the ingredients. Seal and shake to coat thoroughly. Allow to marinate for 10 minutes, turning after 5 minutes. Remove the apple slices and dry with paper towels; discard the marinade. Place a wire rack on a baking sheet and place the apple slices on the wire rack. Bake for 2½ to 3 hours, or until leathery in texture, turning the apple slices over every hour. Allow to cool completely and serve, or store in an airtight container.

DID YOU KNOW . . .

we can make dried fruits live longer by storing them in an airtight container in the fridge? That way they can last for over a year!

Granola Breakup

about 8 cups

With just three ingredients and very little time, we can make this perfect topping for ice cream or yogurt. And the best part is, since it's already broken into pieces, it travels well!

1 box (16 ounces) granola with almonds and raisins
1½ cups lightly salted peanuts
1 can (14 ounces) sweetened condensed milk

Preheat the oven to 300°F. Coat a large rimmed baking sheet with nonstick cooking spray. In a large bowl, combine all the ingredients; mix well. Spread the granola mixture evenly over the baking sheet and bake for 35 to 40 minutes, or until golden. Allow to cool for 5 minutes, then invert onto a clean work surface. Allow to cool completely, then break into bite-sized pieces. Serve, or store in an airtight container.

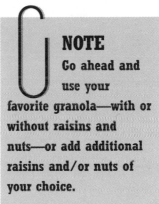

NOTE
Go ahead and use your favorite granola—with or without raisins and nuts—or add additional raisins and/or nuts of your choice.

DID YOU KNOW . . .

sweetened condensed milk is whole milk with 60 percent of its water removed and sugar added?

Homemade Brownies

9 to 12 brownies

One of the most popular foods to send through the mail is brownies, and if they're not wrapped right, they usually end up a big mess by the time they get where they're going. I've found that the trick is to make a moist type of brownie that's not overbaked. And to ensure they don't break, wrap them together in small bundles and pack them all in a sturdy box. Then all that's needed is the right address and the correct postage!

⅓ cup butter
2 squares (1 ounce each) unsweetened chocolate
1¼ cups firmly packed light brown sugar
2 eggs
¾ cup all-purpose flour
¼ teaspoon salt
1 teaspoon vanilla extract
½ cup chopped walnuts (optional)

Preheat the oven to 350°F. Coat an 8-inch square baking dish with nonstick cooking spray. In a small saucepan, melt the butter and chocolate over low heat, stirring frequently. Remove from the heat and set aside. In a large bowl, with an electric beater on medium speed, beat the brown sugar and eggs for 2 to 3 minutes, or until creamy. Add the flour, salt, and the chocolate mixture; beat until well mixed. Stir in the vanilla and the walnuts, if desired. Pour the batter into the baking dish and bake for 30 to 35 minutes, or until set and a wooden toothpick inserted in the center comes out clean. Allow to cool completely, then cut into squares and serve.

NOTE
Wrap each brownie individually in plastic wrap and use fun stickers to seal. Then ship them off to that special someone.

DID YOU KNOW . . .

it's a good idea to stock up on chocolate at after-holiday sales? We can usually get good buys on it after Easter and Christmas, then have it on hand for using in our recipes all year long.

Jelly Bean Brittle

about 2½ pounds

Imagine one sure thing that could be sent any time of the year to say, "Thinking of you." I've got it! Jelly Bean Brittle! It's really versatile 'cause we can use pastel jelly beans for Easter, green and white for St. Patrick's Day, and red, white, and blue for July 4th. So get going and "brittle it" all through the year. And when we want to ship it, it can go right in a decorative tin with some colorful tissue paper, as shown on color page N.

1½ cups miniature jelly beans
3 cups sugar
1 cup light corn syrup
½ cup water
3 tablespoons butter
2 teaspoons baking soda
½ teaspoon salt

Line a large rimmed baking sheet with aluminum foil and coat the foil with nonstick cooking spray. Spread the jelly beans evenly over the foil. In a soup pot, combine the sugar, corn syrup, and water. Bring to a boil over medium heat; without stirring, boil for 10 to 12 minutes, or until the syrup begins to turn golden and reaches the hard crack stage (see Note). Remove from the heat and immediately stir in the butter, baking soda, and salt (the mixture will foam). Continue stirring for 4 to 5 minutes, or until the mixture is shiny. Pour over the jelly beans and spread quickly with a spatula that has been coated with nonstick cooking spray. Allow to cool completely, then invert onto a clean work surface. Remove the foil, then break into bite-sized pieces. Serve, or store in an airtight container.

DID YOU KNOW . . .

jelly beans are simply boiled sugar and fruit flavoring set with gelatin?

NOTE

To test for the hard crack stage: Drop a bit of the mixture from a teaspoon into a glass of cold water. If it forms a strand and hardens in the water, it has reached the hard crack stage. If not, continue to cook the mixture, then test it again after a bit.

Cookie Mailing Tips

Like any other precious cargo, our cookies need special attention so they can travel safely. After all, we put lots of time and care into making them, so we want each of them to arrive at their destination in one piece, instead of ending up a pile of crumbs. Here's what I've found works best:

- Round cookies travel best. Cookies that have points are more apt to break during travel. Avoid sending short-bread-type cookies if possible, since they're brittle. Avoid shipping cookies that have delicate icings and decorations that may smear or smudge during travel.
- Bars and brownies travel well, as do moist cookies. If shipping both crisp and moist cookies, wrap them separately so that each retains its own texture.
- For easier packing, wrap cookies in small bunches, rather than in one large bundle.
- Pack bunches of cookies in a sturdy box, cookie tin, or large coffee can to help them retain their shape and freshness.
- Place heavy cookies on the bottom of the package and lighter cookies on the top.
- Wrap cookies snugly in the package to avoid excessive movement.
- Choose an appropriate cushion for packaging, such as paper towels, waxed paper, shredded paper, or popped popcorn (*unbuttered*). I recommend enclosing a note saying to discard the popcorn after unpacking, since it was used for shipping purposes only.

- There's less breakage if you send several smaller packages (five pounds or under), rather than one large package of goodies.
- Seal the package with shipping tape. Wrap the outside of each package with plain heavy mailing paper or a cut-up brown grocery bag.
- Print the mailing and return addresses clearly with a permanent ink pen or marker so they won't smear if the package gets wet.
- For prompt, safe delivery, mark the package "Perishable—Food" and mark the top "This Side Up."
- Check with your local carrier as to the quickest, safest recommended shipping method for your package.

Looking Good

Over the years, both at QVC and on my daily television vignette, I've shared thousands of recipes with my viewers. And you probably know by now that you can always count on Mr. Food recipes to be quick and easy and to use ingredients that are easily found in your local supermarket. I mean, who wants to run all over town hunting down an exotic ingredient for a recipe? I don't, and I bet you don't, either. I also like to make sure that my recipes look as good as they taste. As the saying goes, we eat with our eyes. So I've devoted an entire chapter to ideas that'll make all our food look extra good. I've even given a quick recipe for each one. No, you won't need any fancy equipment, 'cause it's all so simple! After you try these little tips, everybody's going to be saying this about how your dishes look, not just how they taste: "OOH IT'S SO GOOD!!®"

Looking Good

Looking Good

LIVE from QVC!

M

Jelly Bean Brittle

Chocolate
Chip Biscotti

Cinnamon Coffee Mix

N

"Picture Perfect®"
Homemade Peanut Butter Cups

Chocolate-Almond
Caramel Apples

0

Dreamy Chocolate
Mousse Cake

P

Pepperoni Pizza Dip

6 to 8 servings

Ever heard the expression, "That was so good, I could have eaten the bowl"? Well, sometimes we can do just that. That's right, we can serve food in edible containers. How about a veggie dip in a red bell pepper or our favorite salad served in a cabbage leaf? And then there's always the favorite—a crunchy bread bowl to hold almost anything from thick and creamy soups to hearty dips. Start by hollowing out a loaf of bread, as we do here, and find out how easy it really is.

NOTE
It's a good idea to cut a second loaf of bread into chunks to make sure you have enough for dipping, and when you get to the bottom . . . go ahead and eat the "bowl"!

1 jar (28 ounces) spaghetti sauce
2 cups (8 ounces) shredded mozzarella cheese
1 package (3½ ounces) sliced pepperoni, chopped
½ teaspoon garlic powder
½ teaspoon dried oregano
1 can (2.25 ounces) sliced black olives (optional)
One 1-pound round loaf Italian bread, unsliced

DID YOU KNOW . . .
pepperoni is simply a beef and pork sausage flavored with red and black peppers?

In a medium saucepan, combine all the ingredients except the bread over low heat. Cook for 25 to 30 minutes, or until smooth and creamy, stirring occasionally. Meanwhile, slice the top off the bread and hollow it out, reserving the insides; cut the reserved bread into chunks. Pour the warm dip into the bread bowl and serve with the bread chunks.

Savory Smoked Salmon Cheesecake

6 to 8 servings

We all love surprises, especially when they're served on our plates. One time I made a meat loaf and frosted it with mashed potatoes. It looked just like a cake and sure confused the gang . . . but after one bite, they loved it. Here's another one. How about salmon cheesecake? I know, cheesecake is traditionally topped with chocolate or fruit and served for dessert, but this tasty appetizer will surprise them again and again.

1½ cups finely crushed butter-flavored crackers
¼ cup (½ stick) butter, melted
½ cup (2 ounces) finely shredded Cheddar cheese
2 packages (8 ounces each) cream cheese, softened
3 eggs
2 garlic cloves, minced
¼ teaspoon salt
⅛ teaspoon black pepper
1 package (3 ounces) smoked salmon, chopped

Preheat the oven to 350°F. In a medium bowl, combine the crushed crackers, butter, and Cheddar cheese; mix well and press into a 9-inch pie plate, covering the bottom and sides to form a crust. In a large bowl, with an electric beater on medium speed, beat the cream cheese, eggs, garlic, salt, and

246

pepper until well combined. Reserve half of the mixture; combine the salmon with the other half, mix well, and spoon into the prepared crust. Top with the reserved cream cheese mixture; smooth the top. Bake for 25 to 30 minutes, or until firm in the center. Remove from the oven and allow to sit for 15 to 20 minutes. Serve warm, or cover and chill for at least 4 hours to serve cold.

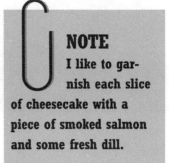

NOTE
I like to garnish each slice of cheesecake with a piece of smoked salmon and some fresh dill.

DID YOU KNOW . . .

dried-on egg comes off silverware more easily with cold water than hot?

Stacked Pasta Salad

8 to 10 servings

Lately it seems that with food, taller is better. The higher it stacks on our plates, the happier we are. I mean, who doesn't love a double or even triple burger and a mile-high ice cream sundae for dessert? That extra layer is a special touch with not much extra work. So here's a stackable salad that tastes just as good as it looks. Oh—don't worry if you cook a few extra veggies or pasta for it . . . just keep layering!

    1 pound pasta twists
    1 container (16 ounces) sour cream
    1 cup mayonnaise
    ½ cup milk
    4 scallions, chopped
    1 tablespoon dried tarragon
    2 teaspoons salt
    1½ teaspoons black pepper
    2 bunches broccoli, cut into small florets and blanched
        (see Note)
    1 large head cauliflower, cut into small florets and
        blanched (see Note)
    1 large red bell pepper, diced

Cook the pasta twists according to the package directions; drain, rinse, and drain again. In a large bowl, combine the sour cream, mayonnaise, milk, scallions, tarragon, salt, and black pepper; mix well. Reserve 1 cup of the sour cream

248

mixture and add the pasta to the remaining sour cream mixture; toss until well coated. In a trifle dish or a large glass serving bowl, layer half the pasta mixture, half the broccoli, half the cauliflower, and half the bell pepper. Repeat the layers once more and drizzle with the reserved sour cream mixture. Cover and chill for at least 2 hours before serving. Toss just before serving.

NOTE
To blanch the broccoli and cauliflower, after they've been cut, just add each to boiling water for 1 minute, then remove to a bowl of ice water to stop the cooking; drain.

DID YOU KNOW . . .

at full capacity, QVC, Inc. can handle one hundred thousand calls per hour? Can you imagine?!

Orange-Glazed Cornish Hens

4 to 8 servings

If you're like me, at one time or another you've opened the oven and decided that something about your roast or chicken was just blah-looking! Well, no more. This easy glaze (made without the Cornish hens, of course) can turn any "okay" dish into "awesome."

    1 medium orange, quartered
    4 Cornish hens
    ½ teaspoon salt
    ¼ teaspoon black pepper
    1 package (4-serving size) orange-flavored gelatin
    ½ cup firmly packed light brown sugar
    ¼ cup orange juice

NOTE
For a really elegant presentation, garnish each serving with the grated rind of a fresh orange.

Preheat the oven to 350°F. Coat a roasting pan with non-stick cooking spray. Place an orange quarter into the cavity of each Cornish hen and place them in the pan. Season with salt and pepper. In a small bowl, combine the remaining ingredients and pour the mixture over the hens. Roast, uncovered, for 1¼ to 1½ hours, or until no pink remains and the juices run clear, basting every 20 minutes. Serve whole or cut each Cornish hen in half, and serve with additional glaze from the pan spooned over the top.

DID YOU KNOW . . .

this easy way to soften brown sugar that has hardened? Simply place a slice of bread in the container and pop it in the microwave for 15 seconds. The moisture in the bread will make steam that'll soften the brown sugar.

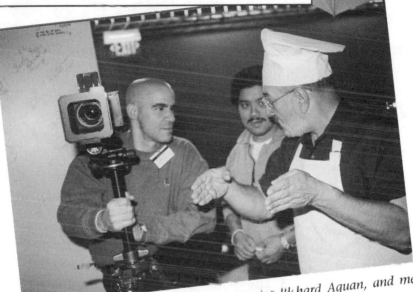

It's photographer Michael Britto, art director Richard Aquan, and me going over details for the book jacket photo shoot.

Stuffed Crown Roast of Lamb

3 to 4 servings

When most of us think about food that's stuffed, we automatically think of turkey. Well, guess what! There are so many other things we can stuff. How about pizza bread stuffed with cheese and pepperoni, or even a jelly roll, which is nothing more than cake stuffed with our favorite jam or jelly? Stuffing adds a special touch, as with this lamb. It gives it real down-home flavor that's far from ordinary in taste *and* appearance.

> One 2½- to 3-pound crown roast of lamb (see Note)
> 1 tablespoon vegetable oil
> 1 teaspoon garlic powder
> 1 teaspoon salt
> ½ teaspoon black pepper
> 3 tablespoons chopped fresh mint (see Note)
> 1 package (8 ounces) corn bread stuffing mix, mixed according to the package directions
> 1 pint small cherry tomatoes

Preheat the oven to 325°F. Coat a roasting pan with nonstick cooking spray; place the roast in the pan. In a small bowl, combine the oil, garlic powder, salt, and pepper; mix well and rub over the entire roast. Add the mint to the corn bread stuffing and cook according to the package directions. Spoon the stuffing mixture into the cavity of the

252

roast. Protect the ends of the rib bones from overbrowning by wrapping them in aluminum foil. Roast for 1 to 1¼ hours, or until a meat thermometer registers 160°F. for medium, or until desired doneness beyond that. Place on a serving platter and let sit for 15 to 20 minutes before serving. Remove the aluminum foil and top each rib bone with a cherry tomato. Place the remaining cherry tomatoes around the roast. Slice the roast between the rib bones and serve with the stuffing.

NOTE
You can ask your supermarket butcher to prepare a crown roast for you. Before serving, be sure to discard any string that may have been used to tie the roast together.

DID YOU KNOW . . .

fresh herbs can really make a dish come alive? Even if a recipe calls for dried herbs, we can substitute using this general rule: 1 teaspoon of dried herb equals 1 tablespoon of the same fresh herb, chopped.

Chicken with Chilled Cranberry Salsa

6 servings

Have you ever mixed hot and cold foods in one dish? Here's a zippy one—chilled salsa spooned over hot chicken. The contrast in taste and temperature is what's so HOT, HOT, HOT today and it works well with so many other food combos, too!

1½ cups fresh cranberries
½ small green bell pepper
½ small onion
¼ cup sugar
2 tablespoons fresh lime juice
1 teaspoon grated lime rind
¼ teaspoon ground ginger
¾ teaspoon salt, divided
6 boneless, skinless chicken breast halves (1½ to 2 pounds total)
¼ teaspoon black pepper
1 tablespoon olive oil
Juice of 1 lemon

Place the cranberries, green pepper, and onion in a food processor and process until finely chopped. Place in a medium bowl and stir in the sugar, lime juice, lime rind, ginger, and ¼ teaspoon salt. Cover and chill for at least 1 hour. Season the chicken with the remaining ½ teaspoon

254

salt and the black pepper. Heat the oil in a large skillet over medium heat. Cook the chicken for 3 to 4 minutes per side, or until no longer pink. Stir in the fresh lemon juice and cook for 1 minute. Serve the chicken topped with the chilled cranberry salsa.

DID YOU KNOW . . .

to determine if cranberries are good, besides the fact that they should be hard and bright, the berries should bounce?

255

Roasted Prime Rib

4 to 6 servings

Not only did I grow up the son of a butcher, but I became one, too. So I know a thing or two about carving the turkeys, roasts, and other poultry and meat cuts that we all enjoy so much. And let me tell you, carving is easier than it looks. With a few simple tips, we can all carve like pros. But first we've gotta have that masterpiece to serve, so here it is. Oh—don't forget the garnish, 'cause that's what makes the platter picture-perfect.

> One 4- to 5-pound beef rib eye roast
> 3 tablespoons vegetable oil
> 1 tablespoon dried parsley flakes
> 1½ teaspoons garlic powder
> 1 teaspoon onion powder
> 1½ teaspoons salt
> 1½ teaspoons black pepper
> 4 cherry tomatoes, cut in half
> 1 ear fresh or thawed frozen corn, cut into eight ½-inch
>   slices

Preheat the oven to 350°F. Coat a large roasting pan with nonstick cooking spray; place the roast fat side up in the pan. In a small bowl, combine the oil, parsley, garlic powder, onion powder, salt, and pepper; mix well. Rub evenly over the roast. Roast for 1½ to 1¾ hours, or until a meat

256

thermometer reaches 140°F. for medium-rare, or until desired doneness beyond that. Allow to sit for 15 minutes, then place on a serving platter. Place a tomato half over the center of each corn slice, creating "daisies" to place around the roast as a garnish.

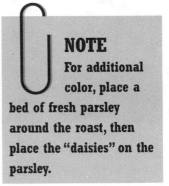

NOTE
For additional color, place a bed of fresh parsley around the roast, then place the "daisies" on the parsley.

DID YOU KNOW . . .

certain herbs are best matched with certain meats?

For example, the best herbs to partner with beef are

basil, thyme, sweet marjoram, and savory rosemary.

Step right up and get your tickets! The QVC Studio Tour starts here with a big smile from Candy Badzik.

Meat Carving Tips

- Make sure that your roast is cooked to the proper doneness. If it's too rare, it will be difficult to carve. And if it's overcooked, it might be tough or too tender, making it fall apart when you cut it.

- Let a roast sit out of the oven in the roasting pan for 10 to 15 minutes after cooking so that the cooking process can finish.

- Place the item to be carved on a clean cutting board that is bigger than the item. Be sure it sits solidly on the board and does not wobble. Cutting boards with a well or a ridged edge work great for roasts since they collect the juices that run off during carving. I also prefer boards without prongs; that way the meat can be moved as each slice is carved.

- Use a sharp knife with an 8- to 10-inch blade for carving roasts, and a knife with a smaller blade for cutting steaks. It's important to keep knives sharp, and there's such a variety of knife sharpeners available today that it's not hard to do.

- A 2-pronged kitchen fork is helpful for holding meat in position while carving, and also for removing sliced meat from the board. The fork should not be repeatedly inserted into the meat because piercing it allows the flavorful juices to escape.

- You can carve your meat either in the kitchen or at the

dining table, but wherever it's done, make sure there's enough room to maneuver. Also, have your serving platter handy to collect the carved slices as they're ready.

- If you have a bone-in roast, cut along the bone of the roast, then carve toward the bone.
- Cut larger roasts and steaks across the grain with your knife blade at a slight angle. This will give you larger, more tender slices. So, what does "cut across the grain" mean, anyway? It refers to the direction the meat should be carved in relation to the direction of the natural meat fibers. The fibers generally run through the meat all in the same direction, except in certain cuts like brisket, where the grain changes directions. So check the direction of the fibers before you begin carving . . . and instead of carving parallel to them, cut across them at an angle.
- If your roast is held together with string or skewers, remove them carefully as you carve. This helps keep the meat from falling apart.
- Carve just the amount of meat that you'll need for your meal. If you leave the rest of it whole, it'll stay moister for the next meal.
- Before serving, spoon or pour some pan drippings or sauce over the carved slices . . . and enjoy!

So-Colorful Fruit Tart

12 to 16 servings

When we start cooking, one of the most important things to remember is that if our finished dish doesn't look good, people won't want to eat it. And nothing makes food more appetizing than a splash of color. It can be just about anything from a dash of paprika on our potatoes to chopped red bell peppers in our macaroni salad. A bit of color makes plain old ho-hum a bit more special . . . like this tart. Top it off with a rainbow of colorful fresh fruit and you'll see what I mean.

1 package (20 ounces) refrigerated sugar cookie dough, cut into ½-inch slices
1 package (4-serving size) instant vanilla pudding and pie filling
1½ cups cold milk
1 kiwi, peeled and sliced
1 can (15¼ ounces) sliced peaches, drained
1 pint fresh blueberries, washed
1 pint fresh strawberries, washed, hulled, and halved
¼ cup apricot preserves
1 tablespoon water

Preheat the oven to 350°F. Coat a 12-inch pizza pan with nonstick cooking spray; place the cookie slices on the pan. With lightly floured hands, press the dough together to

260

form one large cookie the size of the pan. Bake for 9 to 11 minutes, or until the top is light golden. Remove from the oven and allow to cool. In a large bowl, whisk the pudding mix and milk together until thickened. Spread evenly over the cookie dough. Arrange the fruit in a circular pattern over the pudding, beginning with the kiwi in the center, then continuing with the peaches and blueberries, and ending with a border of strawberries. (See the finished tart on color page A.) In a small saucepan, combine the apricot preserves and water over medium heat, stirring until the preserves are melted. Gently brush over the fruit and chill for at least 1 hour before serving. Cut into wedges and serve, or cover and keep chilled until ready to serve.

NOTE
Let your imagination go wild! Almost any of your favorite fresh or frozen fruit, or even some canned fruit, can be used as a substitute for the fresh fruits. Just remember to keep it colorful.

DID YOU KNOW . . .

we can keep sliced fresh fruit from browning and discoloring by sprinkling it with a little lemon or orange juice?

Frozen Strawberry Mousse with Chocolate Drizzle

12 to 16 servings

We can all use a little drizzle in our lives. No, I don't mean rain drizzle, I mean food drizzle. We love to drizzle everything from gravy to salad dressings. But the best drizzle I can think of is chocolate. With just a few strokes, we can turn ordinary into fancy. That's right, drizzling is very popular, and it's easy as pie . . . oops, I mean mousse! Simply fill a clean empty ketchup or mustard squeeze bottle with chocolate sauce (or any sauce!) and give it a squeeze to create a random pattern on the plate or on top of your food. Very fancy looking . . . very easy!

⅓ cup boiling water

2 envelopes (¼ ounce each) unflavored gelatin

1 quart vanilla ice cream, softened

1 cup (½ pint) heavy cream

2 packages (10 ounces each) frozen strawberries in syrup, thawed, 1 package drained

1 package (4-serving size) strawberry gelatin

Chocolate syrup for drizzling

Line a 9" × 5" loaf pan with plastic wrap. In a small bowl, combine the boiling water and unflavored gelatin, stirring until the gelatin has dissolved; set aside to cool slightly. In a blender, combine the ice cream and heavy cream and blend until smooth. Pour the gelatin mixture into the blender and blend until thoroughly combined. Pour half of the mixture into a medium bowl and add the drained strawberries; mix well and set aside. Add the strawberry gelatin and the remaining package of strawberries, with their syrup, to the remaining ice cream mixture in the blender; blend until the strawberries are puréed and the mixture is smooth. Pour half of the mixture into the pan. Smooth the top and freeze for 5 minutes, or until firm. Spread the reserved ice cream mixture in the bowl evenly over that and freeze for 5 minutes, or until firm. Spread the strawberry mixture remaining in the blender over the top and freeze for at least 4 hours, or until firm. Drizzle chocolate syrup on each serving plate and place a slice of the frozen mousse over the syrup. Serve immediately.

NOTE

Be creative when drizzling your plates with the chocolate syrup, and for the finishing touch, garnish each plate with a fresh strawberry.

DID YOU KNOW . . .

16.1 million people have made a purchase from QVC, Inc.? (That's more than the population of the state of Pennsylvania!)

Dreamy
Chocolate Mousse Cake

12 to 16 servings

You've got to admit that with some desserts, the decorations really "take the cake." I often visit my local bakery to get new ideas that I can simplify to keep my cake tops looking good. Of course, then I share them with you. Here's one we can all use to make a plain chocolate mousse cake look like an absolute dream. Wanna see just how dreamy it is? Check it out! It's on color page P. Believe me, it's easy to make and as big on taste as it is on looks.

> 3 cups finely crushed chocolate graham crackers
> ½ cup (1 stick) butter, melted
> 2 eggs
> 4 egg yolks
> 3¼ cups semisweet chocolate chips, divided
> 2 cups (1 pint) heavy cream
> ⅓ cup confectioners' sugar
> 1 package (6 ounces) white baking bars
> ½ teaspoon vegetable shortening

In a medium bowl, combine the crushed graham crackers and butter; mix well. Press into a 10-inch springform pan, covering the bottom and sides to form a crust. Chill until ready to use. In a small bowl, beat the eggs and egg yolks; set aside. In a medium saucepan, melt 3 cups chocolate chips over low heat, stirring constantly. Add the egg mixture, quickly whisking until well blended. Remove from the heat; set aside to cool slightly. Meanwhile, in a medium bowl, with an electric beater on medium speed, beat the heavy cream until soft peaks form. Add the confectioners' sugar and beat until stiff peaks form. Fold the whipped cream into the slightly cooled chocolate mixture until well blended. Spoon into the prepared crust; cover and chill for at least 6 hours, or until firm. Meanwhile, line a rimmed baking sheet with aluminum foil. In a small saucepan, melt the baking bars over low heat, stirring continuously. Spread the melted baking bars into an ⅛-inch-thick layer on the baking sheet. In a small saucepan, heat the remaining ¼ cup semisweet chocolate chips and the shortening over low heat, stirring constantly until melted. Drizzle over the white chocolate. Chill for 30 minutes, or until firm. When ready to serve, break the sheet of chocolate into pieces of varying sizes. Remove the ring from the springform pan and place the cake on a serving platter. Arrange the chocolate pieces so they're sticking out the top of the cake as a garnish (as in the photo, color page P). Slice and serve.

NOTE
If you wanna go just a little further, serve each slice with some fresh whipped cream on the side and a whole strawberry. Wow!

DID YOU KNOW ...

butter is mentioned several times in the Bible? I guess that makes it heavenly ...

In My Travels

For those of you who don't know, QVC is located in West Chester, Pennsylvania, just west of Philadelphia. I visit their studios quite a few times every year and, when time permits, I try to pop into Philly to visit some of the many great restaurants in the area.

And there are lots to choose from! Philadelphia's a real melting pot. From its Italian neighborhoods to Chinatown, street vendors to seafood restaurants, every mouthwatering bite is memorable. So I've included recipes for some of the many different tastes I've tried over the years at Philadelphia's eateries. C'mon and sample away!

In My Travels

In My Travels

Chinatown Garlic Spinach

4 servings

Philadelphia's Chinatown, in the heart of the city, is a great little area to stroll around, shop in, and, of course, eat in! There's one place in particular, Joe's Peking Duck House, that's known for its Peking duck. The dish is so tasty it's not hard to see where their reputation came from! And as a go-along, I often order their garlic spinach. Boy, is it loaded with garlic! Here's my version that's pretty darned close to the original, at least in my opinion.

¼ cup peanut oil
10 garlic cloves, minced
1 tablespoon light soy sauce
¼ teaspoon black pepper
2 packages (10 ounces each) fresh spinach, trimmed, washed, and dried

In a soup pot or wok, heat the oil over medium-high heat. Add the garlic and sauté for 1 minute. Stir in the soy sauce and pepper; mix well. Stir in half of the spinach and cook until just wilted. Stir in the remaining spinach and sauté for 2 to 4 minutes, or until wilted and heated through. Serve immediately.

DID YOU KNOW . . .

Popeye was created by Elzie Crisler Segar in 1919? Because Popeye's extraordinary strength was derived from spinach, it made it easier for moms around the country to persuade their kids to eat the vitamin-packed green veggie.

Peking Chicken

6 to 8 servings

Peking duck is a real delicacy, but with everyone watching their waistlines these days, I decided to make an easy version that's a little leaner because it's made with chicken. The traditional duck recipe requires lots of time-consuming steps, so not only is this version lighter in the fat department, but it's also light on preparation time. And the taste? Not as authentic as in Chinatown, but a pretty good alternative for a busy weeknight supper!

1 scallion, thinly sliced

3 tablespoons soy sauce

2 tablespoons dry sherry

⅓ cup cornstarch

1 teaspoon ground ginger

1 teaspoon sugar

¼ teaspoon white pepper

2 pounds boneless, skinless chicken thighs, cut into 1-inch chunks

2 tablespoons vegetable oil

In a medium bowl, combine the scallion, soy sauce, sherry, cornstarch, ginger, sugar, and pepper; mix well. Add the chicken chunks and toss to coat completely. Cover and marinate in the refrigerator for 3 hours. In a large skillet, heat the oil over medium heat. Remove the chicken chunks from the marinade, discarding the marinade, and cook the chicken in batches for 8 to 10 minutes, or until crispy on all sides and no pink remains.

DID YOU KNOW . . .

Peking Duck is traditionally served with thin pancakes, hoisin sauce, and fresh scallions? Peking Chicken is great that way, too!

Philadelphia Cheese Steak Sandwiches

4 sandwiches

If you ever accompanied me to Philadelphia, you can bet we'd stop at Pat's King of Steaks, where the Philadelphia cheese steak sandwich was born. Pat's is in a small wedge-shaped building in South Philly. I'd order you up a sandwich covered in cheese and piled with toppings, and we'd sit at one of the outdoor tables so we could enjoy the sights, sounds, and smells of South Philly.

        3 tablespoons vegetable oil
        2 large green bell peppers, cut into ¼-inch strips
        2 large onions, thinly sliced
        1¼ pounds beef top round, thinly sliced (see Note)
        ½ teaspoon black pepper
        4 hoagie rolls, split
        ¾ cup Cheese Whiz®, melted

Heat the oil in a large skillet over medium-high heat. Add the bell peppers and sauté for 10 minutes. Add the onions and sauté for 5 to 7 minutes, or until the vegetables are tender. Transfer to a small bowl, cover, and set aside. Add the sliced beef to the skillet and sprinkle with the black pepper; sauté for 3 to 5 minutes, or until the beef is no longer pink. Return the peppers and onions to the skillet and cook for 3 to 5 minutes, or until heated through. Place the beef mixture over the hoagie rolls, drizzle with the melted cheese, and serve immediately.

DID YOU KNOW . . .

Pat's original steak sandwich was created in 1930, but cheese wasn't added until 1948?

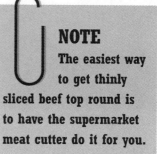

NOTE
The easiest way to get thinly sliced beef top round is to have the supermarket meat cutter do it for you.

Desmond Veal Oscar

6 servings

Whenever I travel, it feels good to see a familiar face or name. Imagine my surprise the first time I saw the Desmond Hotel and Conference Center in Great Valley, since I knew the food so well from the Desmond in Albany, New York, my hometown area. This Desmond's restaurant is also as nice as its friendly staff. Among the many items on the menu there are two that pop into my mind as my favorites . . . bread pudding and veal Oscar. Unfortunately, I wasn't able to get the pudding recipe, but they shared the basics for their classic Oscar. I did simplify it a bit to make it at-home easy.

½ cup all-purpose flour

½ teaspoon salt

¼ teaspoon black pepper

6 veal cutlets (about 1 pound total), lightly pounded

About 2 tablespoons butter

1 package (10 ounces) frozen asparagus spears, thawed and drained

1 can (6½ ounces) lump crabmeat, drained and flaked

¼ cup sour cream

¼ cup mayonnaise

2 teaspoons yellow mustard

1 teaspoon fresh lemon juice

Preheat the oven to 450°F. In a shallow dish, combine the flour, salt, and pepper; mix well. Coat the veal in the flour mixture. In a large skillet, melt 1 tablespoon butter over medium heat. Add the veal in batches and sauté for 1 to 2 minutes, or until lightly golden, turning once and adding more butter as needed. Place the veal in a single layer in a 9" × 13" baking dish. Top each cutlet with an equal amount of asparagus and then crabmeat. In a small bowl, combine the remaining ingredients; mix well and spoon evenly over the crabmeat. Bake for 8 to 10 minutes, or until bubbly and light golden. Serve immediately.

DID YOU KNOW . . .

most canned crab is a mixture of blue crab from the Atlantic Ocean and Gulf of Mexico?

Diner Corned Beef Hash

8 servings

Whenever I appear on QVC, the time schedule is always different. Sometimes I'm on at five o'clock in the morning and other times it's five o'clock in the afternoon. It's nice to know that there are lots of little diners around Philadelphia, and most of them are open around the clock. And, yes, they serve breakfast twenty-four hours a day. So I usually get one of my favorites—diner corned beef hash, made with chopped corned beef and loads of peppers and onions. Here's a shortcut version we can make at home that starts with canned corned beef. It's perfect for serving when the gang pops over or for an anyday brunch.

> ¾ cup (1½ sticks) butter
> 1 large onion, diced
> 1 medium green bell pepper, diced
> 1 package (32 ounces) frozen cubed hash brown potatoes, thawed
> 1 can (12 ounces) corned beef
> 1 tablespoon Worcestershire sauce
> 8 eggs

Preheat the oven to 350°F. Coat a 9" × 13" baking dish with nonstick cooking spray. In a soup pot, melt the butter over medium-high heat. Add the onion and pepper and sauté for 4 to 5 minutes, or until tender. Add the potatoes and cook for 10 to 12 minutes, or until golden, stirring occasionally. Add the corned beef and Worcestershire sauce; mix well and spoon into the baking dish. Using a serving spoon, make eight evenly spaced indentations about ½ inch deep in the mixture (see Note at right and photo on color page C). Crack the eggs one at a time and place an egg in each indentation. Bake for 20 to 25 minutes, or until the eggs are cooked to the desired doneness.

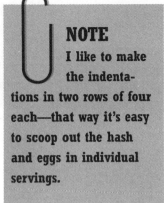

NOTE
I like to make the indentations in two rows of four each—that way it's easy to scoop out the hash and eggs in individual servings.

DID YOU KNOW . . .

there's a whole diner language? Here are just two examples: A "splash of red noise" is a bowl of tomato soup and a "blonde with sand" is coffee with cream and sugar.

Street Vendor Homemade Soft Pretzels

4 pretzels

Philadelphia is known for its open markets and the street vendors who set up on just about every corner. Sometimes when I'm on the plane on my way to Philly, I start thinking about those hot soft pretzels. Lucky for me, I don't have to wait long 'cause there are pretzel carts right in the airport. Because my family got so tired of hearing me talk about them without their being able to taste them, I came up with a homemade version, made with only four ingredients. Serve 'em with your favorite mustard for a tasty low-fat snack.

> 1 pound frozen bread dough, thawed
> 1 egg white
> 1 tablespoon water
> 1 teaspoon kosher (coarse) salt

NOTE For a little variety, you might want to top these with minced onion or garlic salt instead of coarse s[alt]

Coat two large rimmed baking sheets with nonstick cooking spray. Cut the dough into four equal pieces. On a lightly floured surface, roll each piece into a 24-inch rope, then form into a pretzel shape and place on the baking sheets. In a small bowl, beat together the egg white and water, then brush over the top of each pretzel. Sprinkle with the salt. Loosely cover with plastic wrap and set aside in a warm place to rise for 15 minutes. Preheat the oven to 350°F. Remove the plastic wrap and bake for 15 to 17 minutes, or until golden. Serve warm.

Crispy Coconut Shrimp

4 to 6 servings

One night I was ordering dinner at a great seafood restaurant and I overheard someone mention one of the day's specials . . . coconut shrimp. I decided to be adventurous and give it a try. And, boy, was I glad I did! I took their idea and turned it into a recipe you can make at home in no time.

½ cup all-purpose flour
1 tablespoon sugar
1 teaspoon ground red pepper
½ teaspoon salt
2 eggs
2 tablespoons water
2½ cups sweetened flaked coconut
1 pound large shrimp, peeled and deveined, with tails left on
2 cups vegetable oil

In a shallow dish, combine the flour, sugar, ground red pepper, and salt; mix well. In a medium bowl, beat together the eggs and water. Place the coconut in another shallow dish. Coat the shrimp in the flour mixture, then dip in the egg mixture. Roll in the coconut, pressing it firmly onto both sides of the shrimp to coat completely. Heat the oil in a large saucepan over medium heat. Cook the shrimp in batches for 1½ to 2 minutes, or until golden, turning once during cooking. Drain on a paper towel–lined platter. Serve immediately.

DID YOU KNOW . . .
an easy way to break open a coconut is with a clean screwdriver? Just punch holes in the coconut's three eyes, drain the liquid, bang the coconut with a hammer, and voilà! Fresh coconut!

Bookbinder's Sautéed Red Snapper

4 servings

The Old Original Bookbinder's is one of the oldest restaurants in Philly. It's been around since 1865! The locals refer to it as "the world-famous restaurant down by the river." And there's a reason it's been around so long . . . the food is unbeatable! My favorite dish there is the sautéed snapper. I couldn't figure out what made it so tasty, so the folks there were nice enough to share the recipe. Give it a try and see if anybody at your house can figure out their secret ingredient.

¼ cup all-purpose flour
4 red snapper fillets (about 1½ pounds total)
¼ teaspoon salt
¼ teaspoon black pepper
3 tablespoons olive oil
1 cup Bloody Mary mix
¼ cup dry white wine
½ small onion, finely chopped

Place the flour in a shallow dish. Season the fish with the salt and pepper, then dip in the flour, coating completely. In a

280

large skillet, heat the oil over medium-high heat. Place the fish skin side up in the skillet and sauté for 4 to 5 minutes, or until golden. Turn the fish over and pour the remaining ingredients over it. Cook for 4 to 6 minutes, or until the fish flakes easily with a fork and the sauce has thickened. Serve immediately.

DID YOU KNOW . . .

there are a number of variations of the Bloody Mary? You may have heard of the version made without alcohol—it's a Virgin Mary. And when it's made with Japanese sake, it's a Bloody Mary Quite Contrary.

Deep-Dish Sausage Pizza

6 to 8 slices

NOTE
Don't want it too spicy? Use a milder sausage.

With the heavy Italian influence in the Philadelphia area, it's not surprising that there's a pizza parlor on practically every block! And let me tell you, each one is as good as the next. A trip to Philly wouldn't be complete without a deep-dish sausage pizza, so I knew it had to be included here!

1 pound hot Italian sausage, casings removed (see Note)
1 medium green bell pepper, cut into ¼-inch strips
1 small onion, chopped
1 pound store-bought pizza dough
¾ cup pizza or spaghetti sauce
1½ cups (6 ounces) shredded mozzarella cheese

Preheat the oven to 450°F. Coat a 12-inch deep-dish pizza pan with nonstick cooking spray. In a large skillet, cook the sausage, pepper, and onion over medium heat for 6 to 8 minutes, or until no pink remains in the sausage and the vegetables are tender, stirring constantly; drain and set aside. Using your fingertips or the heel of your hand, spread the dough so that it covers the bottom of the pan and comes three quarters of the way up the sides. Spread the spaghetti sauce over the dough; top with the sausage mixture, then the cheese. Bake for 20 to 25 minutes, or until the crust is crisp and brown. Cut and serve.

Stuffed Eggplant

4 servings

With food as good as Philly's Italian food is, I try to sample a different dish each time I'm there. And one of my most recent choices was stuffed eggplant. It was so good, and it's so easy to make that it's become part of my repertoire at home.

2 medium eggplant, cut lengthwise in half
2 tablespoons butter
1 pound ground beef
1 small onion, chopped
1 small red bell pepper, diced
2 garlic cloves, minced
⅓ cup Italian-flavored bread crumbs
1 teaspoon salt
½ cup grated Parmesan cheese

DID YOU KNOW . . . eggplant, which derived its name from its egg-like shape, was introduced to America by Thomas Jefferson?

Preheat the oven to 350°F. Scoop the center out of each eggplant, leaving a ½-inch-thick shell, and dice. Melt the butter in a large skillet over medium heat. Add the ground beef, diced eggplant, the onion, red pepper, and garlic and sauté for 5 to 7 minutes, or until the beef is browned and the vegetables are tender. Remove from the heat and stir in the bread crumbs and salt. Place the mixture in the eggplant shells and place on a rimmed baking sheet. Sprinkle evenly with the cheese, then coat each with nonstick cooking spray. Bake for 60 to 70 minutes, or until the eggplant shells are tender.

Corned Beef and Rye Cheese Fondue

6 to 8 servings

Whenever I appear on QVC, I always show loads of food. My friend Dave Tinsch helps me prepare it. He's a great cook and, when time permits, he and his wife, Tracy, invite me home for dinner or some nibbles. What gracious hosts they are! Once they made this fondue that's so awesome it really stands out in my mind. It tasted just like a Reuben sandwich. Of course, Dave shared the recipe with me. It's a great one for those times when you just can't decide what you feel like nibbling on.

1 pound sliced deli corned beef
1 loaf (1 pound) dark rye bread, cut into 1-inch chunks
3 cups (12 ounces) shredded Swiss cheese
1 tablespoon all-purpose flour
1 teaspoon caraway seeds
¾ cup dry white wine

Roll up each slice of corned beef jelly-roll style and cut into 1-inch pieces. Place each piece on a wooden skewer or fondue fork with a chunk of bread; set aside. In a medium bowl, combine the cheese, flour, and caraway seeds; toss to coat the cheese completely with the flour. In a medium saucepan, heat the wine over medium heat until bubbly. Add the cheese mixture ¼ cup at a time and cook until the cheese has melted and the mixture is thoroughly blended, stirring constantly. Transfer to a fondue pot or a bowl (see Note) and serve with the corned-beef-and-rye skewers for dipping.

DID YOU KNOW . . .

the Reuben sandwich, made with corned beef, Swiss cheese, and sauerkraut on rye bread with Russian dressing, won first prize in the 1956 National Sandwich Contest?

NOTE
If you don't have a fondue pot, place a heat-resistant bowl on a warming tray to keep the fondue warm. And if you buy sliced corned beef brisket, since it's already narrow, there's no need to cut it into strips. Simply roll up the slices and skewer!

285

Index

Isn't it time to add these other quick, easy, and fun **Mr. Food**® Cookbooks to your collection?

(You can—just call 800-345-1515 and use the order numbers below.)

Mr. Food® Cooks Like Mama
The **Mr. Food**® Cookbook, *OOH IT'S SO GOOD!!*®

F3823

Mr. Food® Cooks Chicken
Mr. Food® Cooks Pasta
Mr. Food® Makes Dessert

F2545

Mr. Food® Cooks Real American
Mr. Food®'s Favorite Cookies

F5426

Mr. Food®'s Old World Cooking Made Easy
"Help, **Mr. Food**®! Company's Coming!"

F1069

To order additional copies of
Mr. Food® A Taste of QVC:
Food & Fun Behind the Scenes,
call QVC at (800) 345-1515
and request item # F18698

Mr. Food® Meat Around the Table
Mr. Food® Pizza 1-2-3
Mr. Food® Simply Chocolate

F9843

Mr. Food® From My Kitchen to Yours:
   Stories and Recipes from Home
Mr. Food® A Little Lighter

F7459

Mr. Food® Easy Tex-Mex
Mr. Food® One Pot, One Meal
Mr. Food® Cool Cravings: Easy Chilled
   and Frozen Desserts

F16242

Mr. Food®'s Italian Kitchen
Mr. Food®'s Simple Southern Favorites

F17577